# So Many Friends,
## So Little Friendship

E H I H I  A .  D O M I N I O N

WESTBOW
P R E S S®
A DIVISION OF THOMAS NELSON
& ZONDERVAN

Scripture taken from the King James Version of the Bible.

Scripture taken from the Amplified Bible, Copyright © 1954, 1958, 1962,
1964, 1965, 1987 by The Lockman Foundation. Used by permission.

WestBow Press books may be ordered through booksellers or by contacting:

WestBow Press
A Division of Thomas Nelson & Zondervan
1663 Liberty Drive
Bloomington, IN 47403
www.westbowpress.com
1 (866) 928-1240

ISBN: 978-1-5127-6030-9 (sc)

Library of Congress Control Number: 2016917016

Print information available on the last page.

WestBow Press rev. date: 11/21/2016

# CONTENTS

# DEDICATION

**This book is dedicated to my Dear departed mother. Mrs. Yemisi Justina Ehihi**

# ACKNOWLEDGEMENT

Giving all glory to God, I genuinely appreciate and profoundly acknowledge the HOLY SPIRIT, my supreme Master, for the inspiration and the ability to write as I receive from Him.
He alone has made it possible for me to sit for hours to receive from Him. His name is praised forever!

With all love and adoration, I appreciate my beautiful wife, **Olubunmi Precious Ehihi,** for all her love and support. I also appreciate Mr. Okpeki Eric Eseosa and Mr. Bright Benson, who support and motivates me during this project.

With all sincerity, I also acknowledge my wonderful parents **(Hon. & late Mrs. Ehihi S.O.)** for their loving parental care against all the odds, and for showing me the way of the Lord right early. Mum and Dad, you will enjoy all the fruit of your labor in Jesus' name.

# INTRODUCTION

## FRIENDS

Old English FRĒOND in Middle English FREND, also in Old English FRĒON, which means to love. FRĒO means free, from the Germanic origin; it is related to Dutch VRIEND and German FREUND, also from an Indo-European root meaning 'to love.' From its origin, we discover that friend means to love and to be loved.

Definitions; From the Dictionary's perspective, a friend is supposed to be a person with whom you have a strong bond of mutual affection with, typically, platonic in nature or one exclusive of family relations. A friend should be one attached to you by affection, esteem or common end.

Considering other views of life, a friend could be seen as someone you love and who loves you as well, that person you respect so well, and who respect you as well, someone who you both trust each other. A friend should be honest always and should make you want, to be frank too. A friend should be loyal likewise you, no matter the situation in which you both find yourselves.

# FRIENDSHIP

**Friendship** is a relationship that has to do with mutual affection between two or more persons. It is a stronger bond or a form of interpersonal relationship than a mere association. Friendship has long time been a prevalent study within academic fields such as psychology, sociology, philosophy and so many on. Studies from a world happiness database actually found that individuals with close friendships are healthier and happier.

There are many forms of friendship, some may vary from one location to another, and some varies in a behavioral order and some in the individual type. Some essential characteristics such as, to mention but a few, altruism, trust, expression of one's feeling, mutual understanding, affection, compassion, sympathy, empathy, ability to express oneself without fear of judgment, and above all love can be found in Friendship.

Even though there had been no limit of any kind on the types of persons that can form a friendship, friendship still tends to share common goals, interest, backgrounds, occupations, or demographics.

A decade ago, there was a study on the American youth, and it was observed that over thousand teenagers in America do engage in a behavioral disorder such as stealing, fighting, violence and truancy, which was related to their friendships. From a close observation, it was noticed that teenagers were less likely to find themselves in behavioral problems when their friends were well behaved in school, involved in various school activities, deserted alcohol and drugs, and are of good mental health. The reverse was noticed in teenagers who did engage themselves in the aforementioned behavioral problems. The truth is that whether the teenagers were influenced by their friends to get themselves involved in behavioral problems greatly depended on their exposure to those type of friends.


## TRUE FRIENDSHIP

I see true friendship as a great and sensational exploit, an ongoing finding of oneself and of one's friends that after a while, if healthy, becomes a quotidian broadening of one's perception, creating an opportunity for learning up-to-the-minute about life, about human way of living and about God. True friendship according to the holy bible, is characterized by love. If you can take your time to read through the book of Proverbs, the example of David and Jonathan in the book of 1Samuel 18, the instructions given to the Church in the New Testament. And above all, the perfect examples our Lord Jesus laid for us to follow, you will have a creative visualization of true friendship. A true friend always loves but not perfect, gives wise counsel always, ever loyal, and forgives even when it seems impossible, promotes and strive for the other's welfare. Your true friends are meant to love at all times [Proverbs 17:17]. Only hurt us in ways that are responsible (i.e., tough love), sometimes closer and more loyal than family relations [Proverbs 18:24], provide and promotes mutual edification, sharpens the countenance of his friends [Proverbs 27:17], can impact wisdom. The scripture also said that he that walks with a wise man will be wise [Proverbs 13:20], and may even have to sacrifice time, substance or themselves for us, greater love hath no man than this, that a man lay down his life for his friends. [John 15:13].

# PONDER POINTS

...............................................................

*If only you can take a meaningful look at those
in your friendship precinct, you will discover
that there lies the direction of your life.*

*The friends we keep go a long way in affecting our
path to the top; they either help us to the mountain
top or bring us down to the deepest valley in life.*

*You will continue to be the same person and will
remain in the same place for years to come except
for these two most important things, your circle
of friends and your sources of information.*

# CHAPTER ONE

*Who Are Your Friends?*

The above question may sound too familiar, or maybe too easy to answer. I love this old time saying which I believe is by the Scripture (proverb 13:20) which goes, Show me your friends, and I will tell you who you are.

It is crucial that you think deeply before answering the above question because you may not have previously understood the great difference between true friends and flakes [wrong friends]. I know if I should be physically asking you this question, you may have a lot of names or pictures to answer me with; some of them may be grouped as your special friends, and some, casual friends or you may refer some as just friends. The truth here is that these people in your life are either right for you, or they are bad for you. In other words, they are either friends or flakes.

Just to let you know before we continue, I am not here to discourage you from having friends or making friends. My message here is to only ensure that you are keeping good friends that actually care about you, as this can foster healthy relationships. According to studies, a healthy relationship is one of the greatest factors for healthy living. It is of essence that we understand the various implications of friendship, its consequences in our life since association can pave the way for a deleterious assimilation. Remember, disreputable companionship will contaminate a well-brought-up individual.

I am also bringing this to your understanding that you can never be different from your friends or the people you always hang out with. I remember my mom always said, "Birds of the same feather flock together in the same direction" whenever she saw me with people she didn't approve of. To be honest with you, that saying is practically true. The friends we keep can go a long way as a major factor to determine how great or how insignificant you will become in life. The earlier you realize this, the better for you because they will affect your path to the top no matter who you are, where you are, or what you aspire to become in life. Your future or destiny may be in great jeopardy if you have bad friends or flakes disguising themselves as your buddies, like wolves in sheep's clothing.

Trust me; friends will either influence you positively or negatively. They are capable of launching you into the circle of great men or into the circle of frustrated fellows, which I refer to as the pit of life.

Friends happen to be a major factor that determines whether or not you will ever fulfill your destiny, whether or not you will enjoy the fullness of the only life you've got to live.

Be it right or wrong friends, male or female, old or young, they never stop influencing you in one way or the other. The sad thing is that we human beings are so quick to imitation and adapt quickly to the evil or sinful lifestyle of our so-called friends. Association can bring about assimilation. It's so shocking to discover that, soon after we spend some time with someone, we find ourselves, unconsciously, mimicking their behavior or idiosyncrasies. Most times we don't even have to be with them long enough before we start making hand gestures like them, or saying their favorite cliché, or making a facial expression the way they do. We, in essence, absorb and conform to their behavior. We are often ignorant of this because most of us just live life without paying attention to details, or maybe because we are not just observant enough to know what is going on in our life. Most of us just live a care-free life or live with what I term an "I don't care" attitude.

It is not at all times easy to know what type of relationship we are in since it is tough for us to recognize and realize that a particular friend is right or just a flake, most especially if you are the type that pays no attention to details.

Here are selected tips you can use to evaluate your friendship or relationship. It is as simple as asking yourself these questions:

- Do your friends make you feel good?
- Do you ever wonder if your friends say negative things about you behind your back?
- Do your friends say negative things about other people behind their back?
- Do your friends ever request you to do things that you are not comfortable with?
- Do your friends make you feel like you are not as good as they are?
- Do your friends like it when you hang out with other people without them?
- Do your friends ask you to contribute more to the relationship?
- Do your friendships make you feel safe and comfortable?
- How much do you trust your friends?
- How much do you think they believe you?
- What have you gained or lost so far in this friendship of yours?
- Above all, does your friendship glorify God?

By examining yourself with these questions, you will start thinking critically about the kind of friends you've been keeping; and after reading this chapter, you will know if it is worth keeping them in your life.

While you are still asking and thinking, let me help you further by simply differentiating between the good friends [real friends] and the wrong friends [flakes].

## FLAKES

*An ungodly man diggeth up evil: and in his lips, there is as a burning fire. A froward man soweth strife: and a whisperer separateth chief friends. A violent man enticeth his neighbor and leadeth him into the way that is not good. He shutteth his eyes to devise froward things: moving his lips he bringeth evil to pass. [proverb 16:26-30]*

Just as it sounds, a flake is flaky, shady, deceitful, unreliable and selfish in nature. These ill characteristics are made either by choice, nature or nurture. People that fall in this category are feeble in nature, they lack discipline, self-control, morals, and salvation. They mostly become friends with people because of what they can benefit or steal e.g. your valuables, attention, fame, money, comfort, and convenience. Their principal objective is what they want to do as if life is all about them. They will cause you much grief, anger, and frustration than you can ever imagine. They don't value those they associate with; they are the type that will run away from the scene of the accident. Flakes are superb at making plans and promises but atrocious at keeping them. They may make their friends feel good in private, but in public, they will embarrass or give them the ignominy of their life just to make them look bad in the presence of people. They always take advantage of their friends and will never see anything good in their buddies. They will demean and belittle your accomplishment. Fake friends backbite, snitch, gossip, ridicule and destroy those that regard them as their friends most especially in their absence. Just like the water, they are unstable and can be manipulative, domineering and erratic in relationships. They never admit faults, also never feel remorse for their wrongdoings. They are great pretenders who will never like to see you succeed since they don't strive for success anyway. Fake friends are phonies. Just like the devil, their mission in your life is to steal, kill and to destroy. They will not stop until they either ruin you or see you come to disaster These type of people cannot keep a relationship due to their way of life. Question or advise them and see how quick and easy they'll get rid of you and move on to another ignorant and available person. In several places in the scripture, they are referred to as fools, unreliable, ungodly, frowardness and so on.

Their ways are full of deceit, regrets, and confusion. They always like associating with things that are immoral and sinful, because that is where they derive their pleasure. They don't appreciate you in any definite form, but rather they depreciate you in value. They do all they can just to hold you down at the bottom because they know that if you make it to the top, there is no room for them there. They have all the necessary tools to distract you from your purpose in life. In many ways they become a nuisance to your life; they even cause you to be very far from God. When you walk in the gathering of those kinds of people, you suffer from things you are not guilty of. You are judged and castigated in many ways as a result of your bad companions. There is this warning proverb my father always had me read as part of my scripture memorization:

> *"Make no friendship with an angry man and with a furious man thou shall not go lest thou learn his ways and get a snare to thy soul."*
>
> *[Proverbs 22:24, 25]*

Flakes here are referred to as angry men, and the scripture said that they are fools full of fury, and there is nothing godly, noble, or manly about them, no matter how you try to justify their behavior or makes excuses for them. Angry men are regarded as fools. If you want to be a wise man, you will avoid them at all costs, or run the risk of learning their hateful and wicked habits until you destroy yourself.

They will make you lose your integrity, your self-esteem, your respect. When your friends are sorry, you cannot escape been judged by their ways. You can never move forward in life if you don't run away from those kinds of people.

As you are reading this book right now, many people are suffering; some are in jail, and some are on death row, some have been killed, and some are about to die, some have serious diseases, and some are under the wrath of God. This is not necessarily because they are bad or because they planned it that way, but mostly because of the flakes in their lives, they received a judgment they did not deserve. See how the Bible warned us against this kind of people.

> *"Enter not into the path of the wicked,*
> *and go not in the way of evil men, avoid it,*
> *pass not by it, turn from it and pass away.*
> *For they sleep not except they have made*
> *mischief and their sleep is, and their sleep*
> *is taken away unless they cause you to fall.*
> *They eat the bread of wickedness and drink*
> *the wine of violence but the paths of the just*
> *are as the shining light that shineth more*
> *and more until the perfect day."*

*[Proverbs 4:14-17]*

Most of your so-called best friend will ruin your life, marriage, and your blood, sweat, and tears for if you don't withdraw from them.

I advise you to scan through your life thoroughly, use this book as an antivirus to get rid of the flakes in your life as he who walks with wise men, will be wise, but a companion of fools shall be destroyed (Proverbs 13:20).

## TRUE FRIENDS

### HOW DO YOU RECOGNISE A TRUE FRIEND?

A true friend happens to be that person who not only doesn't care about your looks, or how boring you may be, but doesn't even think about it. A friend who forgives you no matter what you do, and who attempts to help you even when they are not knowledgeable about how, someone who also tells you if you're acting stupid, but who doesn't make you feel asinine. A true friend is mostly difficult to come by. As we age in life, we begin to see ourselves drifting away from those we've always known to be our best friends during childhood, teenage years, even during high school and college days. It can be every now and then challenging to find new friends and may even be more demanding to maintain old relationships as we undergo the various stages of life. If you are serendipitous enough to find true friendship in your life, you are fortunate, because most of us make a great effort from day to day to adjust and find one true friend that is real, consistent and constant in our life.

## WHAT CAN YOU LOOK OUT FOR IN A TRUE FRIEND?

A true friend is one that loves unconditionally through thick or thin. One who does not betray the trust of friends irrespective of the situation even if it will be beneficial. Someone that knows you better than you can ever imagine and takes a position in your best interest in the time of crisis. A true friend influences those they associate with to either be like them or better than them. True friends don't get jealous when they see their friends with others, they don't envy the success of their friends instead, they strengthen, encourage and admonish one another to achieve their goals. They don't force themselves on someone neither do they force someone to become their friend.

The life of a true friend is just like the one of Jesus Christ, who has given everyone that's willing, the perfect opportunity for becoming one of his friends. He keeps his promises and tells the truth at all time regardless of what may be going on at that particular time. His word means everything to him as he is committed to his word. Real friends are faithful to their words and to them when they give you their words, they don't deter from them i.e. everything that you say should be a bond.

True friends will never engage in malicious talk, gossip and abusively disparaging speech behind their buddies. They communicate openly with each other making themselves aware of their anger, wrongs, displeasure, grievances, expectations, etc. they address their differences as quickly as possible amicably within themselves, given no room for malice. With true friends, your secret will always remain your secret. With all these are real friends perfect? No, they are not, they only strive for perfection in response to God's word that says *"Be ye, therefore, perfect, even as your Father which is in heaven is perfect"* *[Mathew 5: 48]*.

I learned recently that friendship is not a thing that can be found on the side of the road. Nor can it be gifted by someone. It is a process which goes on as you walk through life. It is not a gift; rather, it's a reward. It is an achievement of your goodness, your unending sacrifices, and your unwavering commitment. It's a feeling that gives you strength, and it is always with you wherever you go. It makes your happiest moment more comfortable and your saddest moment lighter. Your real friends will love you for who you are, in the good times and in the bad times. They can find out about your past and still love you. They are always there to listen to you at any time whether you need to talk, cry or even sing. They will never tell your secret to anyone unless keeping it will endanger your life. They can be truthful with you regardless of the situation, even at the risk of hurting your feelings, they should also be that friend that can sometimes be in disagreement with you and still remain good friends, else wise, they cannot be referred to as a true friend.

They will never gossip about you. Instead, you and your privacy will always be relevant to your buddies. They also stick by you no matter what it will cost them unless you've done them some wrong that can harm their destiny or future. They don't disappear from your life without good reasons. They will always be close to each other either in the distance or by heart. True friends do anything for you unless it is actually unreasonable for them to do it. In other words, they would give you the shirt off their back, if needed.

The are friends that have a kind heart and hold their friends close to it at all times. To be honest with you, friendship is not always something sweet. They are human; they are imperfect beings, and they make mistakes. They can also hurt you the most because they know absolutely everything about you. The good thing is that when they hurt you, they don't just leave you hanging. Most certainly, they apologize if they have wronged you and they always come up with some plans to make it up to you or to make you feel better.

Your real friend is that person you may not see or hang out with for months or longer, but when you finally do meet again, it's like those months never happened. They don't always have to be by your side for you to feel you both get each other right. They are not perfect, but they got you covered as much as they could. I always refer them to be the transcendent kind of friend.

They don't sugar coat important things like that because they do care about your wellbeing, even though the manner in which they present it may be far from the conventional way. Real friends will watch you dance like a maniac in public, but will eventually join you because they don't want you to look like a lunatic all by yourself. They will love you and say it at random times. They are the type that will still be by your side decades from now. You will be old and wrinkled, but you will still be partners for life. They listen to your every word, never interrupting you, no matter how long or how irrelevant your complaints may be.

Lastly, a true friend is someone who calls you now and then asking you how you are doing, and also telling you how much you mean to them, no matter the situation, either directly or indirectly. A friend in need is a friend have to, anytime. Such friends can never be replaced, not even with hundreds of people, no matter how beautiful, good looking, rich or sweet talking.

> *"....and there is a friend that sticks closer than a brother."*
>
> *[Proverbs 18:24b]*

With love, TRUE FRIENDSHIP makes two souls become one, so much that they can often sense what the other person thinks or feels. Many marriages are based on this kind of friendship, and they are the ones that last through the trials and tribulations a relationship may experience. In all, your true friend should be your partner and not your follower or leader.

# PONDER POINTS

...........................................................

*As people will always say "Blood is thicker than water" when choosing family over friends; but, Jonathan even turned his back on his own father for the sake of the friendship, he shared with David. In other words, this type of friendship is "thicker than blood" and "dearer than a brother."*

There is a very dangerous trap... those who... quickly will
between peace and community.

Proverb 16:5 (NIV)?

A true friend is that person in whom you can open your heart.

# CHAPTER TWO

*Friendship According to the Holy Book*

Through thick and thin, both tall and small, during fast and slow. Who do you think will always be there for you? Assuming you don't know. Your best friend, of course, if you have one, don't let go. I know you must have probably met and known diverse people in your life. Most of them may simply be a person you know slightly, but who is not a close friend, while others you might consider friends. Of all these, there may be only a few that you would find close or real friends. In life there is always that person, who is as close to you as a brother or sister, just as the Bible says:

The man of too many friends [chosen indiscriminately] will be broken in pieces and come to ruin,

> *"But there is a [true, loving] friend who [is reliable and] sticks closer than a brother."*

> *[Proverb 18:24 AMP]*

A true friend is that person in whom you can open your heart to, trust and share your visions and dreams without fear. A true friend is one who is always there not only for the good times but also the bad times; someone who won't abandon or desert you when the going gets tough. A true friend is one that withstands the test of trials and time, and this is very rare and hard to find. Friends always come and go, but to have a true, lifelong, close personal friendship is truly a great blessing from God alone. Now that we have been proficient enough to ascertain what we mean by friendship, flakes and true friendship from above; let's take a good look at some examples set before us by the holy book. Since we are children of God, it will be very useful for us to emulate the holy scriptures regarding how to live our life and who to share our life with.

## God and Abraham (faith, obedience, and reward)

The relationship between God and Abraham is one that has to do with faith, reward as a result of obedience. It was clearly stated in the Bible (2 Chronicles 20:7) that Abraham was God's friend. Prophet Isaiah also made it clear in one of his record (Isaiah 41:8), that Abraham was a friend of God. James, who was a servant of God and of the Lord Jesus Christ, in his epistle, confirmed the friendship between God and Abraham.

> *"And the Scripture was fulfilled which says,*
> *"Abraham believed God, and this [faith] was*
> *credited to him [by God] as righteousness*
> *and as conformity to His will," and he was*
> *called the friend of God."*

> *[James 2:23 AMP]*

Their friendship was one that was bounded by an endless faith, sacrifice, and obedience. The Bible did not portray Abraham to be sinless in all form and fashion, but his unending faith in God to take the lead of his life, family and properties made Abraham so exceptional. As seen in several accounts in the Bible, Abraham took delight in obeying the voice of God, regardless of the sacrifices involved. Please don't get it twisted, though Abraham was a friend of God, he did not get his salvation through works, but by his obedience and faith in the promise of God. Apostle Paul made this well-defined in the epistle to the Romans, to clarify that salvation is offered through the gospel of Jesus Christ.

What then shall we say that Abraham, our forefather humanly speaking, has found? [Has he obtained a favored standing?] 2 For if Abraham was justified [that is, acquitted from the guilt of his sins] by works [those things he did that were good], he has something to boast about, but not before God. For what does the Scripture say? "Abraham believed in (trusted, relied on) God, and it was credited to his account as righteousness (right living, right standing with God)." [Romans 4:1-3AMP]

The amazing thing about this friendship was that Abraham's faith in God attracted a reward from God. He was blessed beyond curse, his blessing was spread for generations and generations to come. He experienced a miracle that surpassed medical and human understanding. As a result of his obedience to God, he found favor in the sight of God to be made the father of all nations, even though by then he had no child. In most cases, we claim the blessings of Abraham, but are we ready to apply for the responsibility of faith in God as Abraham? If you are already working on this path of faith and obedience to God, I want to promise you that, there is always a reward for the righteous, both earthly and heavenly.

## The genuine friendship between Jonathan and David (Altruistic and lifesaving relationship)

The unpretentious friendship of Jonathan and David is one that can be seen as self-sacrificing and noble in nature. As you read about this friendship in the Bible (1 Samuel 18-20), you will find that they shared much in common. There were also situations that could have easily wacked their relationship, but instead, put a shine on their friendship. From the story, we could see the relationship between King Saul (first king of Israel), Prince Jonathan (King Saul's son) and David (the shepherd boy). It was part of the tradition then, for Jonathan to be the next king of Israel. King Saul disobeyed God, and as a consequence of his disobedience, the kingdom was taken away from King Saul forever. David, without asking, found favor in the sight of God and was chosen to be the next king of Israel. The alarming success of David and his men in putting an end to the constant oppression coming from the Philistine gave rise to suspicion and jealousy from Saul. This brought enmity between King Saul and David, which also made Saul seek David's life.

> *"As they were coming [home], when David returned from killing the Philistine, the women went out of all the cities of Israel, singing and dancing, to meet King Saul with tambourines, [songs of] joy, and musical instruments. The women sang as they played and danced, saying, "Saul has slain his thousands, and David his ten thousand." Then Saul became furious, for this saying displeased him; and he said, "They have ascribed to David ten thousand, but to me, they have ascribed [only] thousands. Now, what more can he have but the kingdom?" Saul looked at David with suspicion [and jealously] from that day forward."*

> *[1 Samuel 18:6, AMP]*

We could say that Jonathan discerned that David would be the succeeding king, instead of him as the prince, but he made friendship and loved David anyway. It was very evident that the prince was inclined to trust God's decision when it comes to a matter of choosing the next king, with a reasonable understanding that it was the same God that chose his father over others. This also insinuates an acceptance to Jonathan that he would never be king, and his household also may become subject to David when he becomes king. There were some positions where Jonathan had the opportunity to eliminate David, as some of us would, but he chose otherwise.

> *"And Saul spake to Jonathan, his son, and to all his servants, that they should kill David, but Jonathan Saul's son delighted much in David. And Jonathan told David, saying, Saul, my father seeketh to kill thee. Now, therefore, I pray thee, take heed to thyself until the morning, and abide in a secret place, and hide thyself. And I will go out and stand beside my father in the field where thou art, and I will commune with my father of thee; and what I see, that I will tell thee. And Jonathan spake good of David unto Saul, his father, and said unto him, let not the king sin against his servant, against David; because he hath not sinned against thee, and because his works have been to thee-ward very good: For he did put his life in his hand and slew the Philistine, and the Lord wrought a great salvation for all Israel: thou sawest it, and didst rejoice: wherefore then wilt thou sin against innocent blood,*

> *to slay David without a cause? And Saul*
> *hearkened unto the voice of Jonathan: and*
> *Saul sware, As the Lord liveth, he shall not*
> *be slain."*

*[1 Samuel 19:1-6, KJV]*

Jonathan chose to save David's life. At that time, he did all his best as he has promised David to talk to his father, up to the extent of restoring their relationship. And from the scripture above, we could see that he succeeded in convincing his father, pledging never to exterminate David.

There were many times afterward that the King strived to slay David. Instead, Jonathan always aids his escape. There was a time that it became apparent to Jonathan that his father will do anything to kill David, Jonathan had to endanger his own life, so as to defend his friend. Jonathan even went as far as confronting his frightful father regarding David, and at this time, his father's wrath was twirled towards him. Even though they split up ways, in the long run, their separation was out of necessity.

> *"And Jonathan said to David, go in peace,*
> *forasmuch as we have sworn both of us in*
> *the name of the Lord, saying, The Lord*
> *be between me and thee, and between my*
> *seed and thy seed forever. And he arose and*
> *departed: and Jonathan went into the city."*

*[1 Samuel 20:42, KJV]*

They pledged to one another to remain loyal to each other, including their households and kingdoms. Their covenant and the indisputable relationship as seen in the scripture below is a good example of friendship that should be emulated.

> *"And thou shalt not only while yet I live shew me the kindness of the Lord, that I die not: But also thou shalt not cut off thy kindness from my house forever: no, not when the Lord hath cut off the enemies of David everyone from the face of the earth. So Jonathan made a covenant with the house of David, saying, Let the Lord even require it at the hand of David's enemies. And Jonathan caused David to swear again because he loved him: for he loved him as he loved his own soul."*

> *[1 Samuel 20:14-16 KJV]*

David, after the separation, was heartbroken to hear of his beloved friend's death. It was a huge and notable loss for David to listen to the news of Saul and Jonathan's loss of life. He expresses his unpleasant emotions by composing a song, to express his grief, which he titled "the Song of the Bow," he also made sure the song was taught to everyone in Judah. I see this as a breathtaking accolade to a real friend, as many of us would have celebrated and show gratitude to God for the death of their enemies. According to an article published by The Restored Church of God, on Jonathan and David-A True and Lasting Friendship," The record of David and Jonathan's friendship and character has been preserved as lessons in the Bible for our benefit. It gives us the picture of the close relationship between

God the Father and Jesus Christ. They desire that same close, personal relationship with every human being. Jonathan and David's friendship is and will continue to be a lasting legacy.

I believe when David and Jonathan will see each other on the resurrection, it will be just like the last day they saw each other on earth, and they will continue to enjoy a friendship that will last for eternity. You can develop that kind of friendship with God and Christ, and with all others of like mind, who share the same goals, hopes, and dreams. And always remember to find common ground in friendship, because it helps a lot" (RCG, 2013).

In summary, we can say that the friendship between Jonathan and David was altruistic and lifesaving, and the one to model yourself on. Now we can understand where the ponder-point came out from since we always claim "Blood is thicker than water," when choosing family over friends; but, we can see from the story how Jonathan even turned his back on his own father for the sake of the love he shared with his friend. In other words, this type of friendship is "thicker than blood" and "dearer than a brother." These men were so practical and keen to show deep love for one another, making an example of a genuine and lasting friendship. Most of all, David and Jonathan were prepared to lay aside their lives for one another. Their connection was so pronounced in some of their valedictions,

> *"Jonathan gave his weapons to his boy and said to him, "Go, take them to the city." As soon as the boy was gone, David got up from the south side [beside the mound of stones] and fell on his face to the ground [in*

> *submission and respect], and bowed three*
> *times. Then they kissed one another and*
> *wept together, but David wept more."*

> *[I Samuel 20:41, AMP]*

How often can you find this nature of friendship in this present day world full of flakes? The great news here is that it is very possible, first of all, you were destined to have this nature of the relationship with Christ. I will like to refer you to the scripture below:

> *"This is My commandment, that you love*
> *and unselfishly seek the best for one another,*
> *just as I have loved you. No one has greater*
> *love [nor stronger commitment] than to lay*
> *down his own life for his friends. You are my*
> *friends if you keep on doing what I command*
> *you. I do not call you servants any longer, for*
> *the servant does not know what his master*
> *is doing; but I have called you [My] friends*
> *because I have revealed to you everything*
> *that I have heard from My Father."*

> *[John 15:13-15, AMP]*

Secondly, with Christ being your friend, He will Guide and direct your path to those that are like him (hope, vision and drive), since likes attract likes. Christ in you is the hope of glory, the hope of getting new friends, the hope of becoming a true friend to others and lastly the hope of maintaining a true friendship that will last like that of David and Jonathan. In searching for a true friend, and becoming a real friend, it will be of immense help to find common ground when talking about friendship.

## Ruth and Naomi (A bitter and sweet commitment)

This is a story that connotes a painful commitment, that leads to a delightful experience, due to patience. It all started from family marriage relationship, where Ruth's dear departed husband was Naomi's son, and from the story, we could tell they were also friends. Naomi tried to convince Ruth to return to her family since the family bond was no longer there. Ruth, on the other hand, was firm on her vow on returning with Naomi to her native land in Israel, meanwhile, to Ruth the friendship bond was unwavering. It was true that Ruth had suffered the loss of her husband, but she was not willing to also lose her dear friend, Naomi. Eventually, Ruth and Naomi returned back home together grief-stricken and traumatized. The bible recorded that they were devoted and truthful to one another. It was, as a result of her truthfulness and commitment to Naomi, that Ruth found favor and love in the sight of Naomi's family member (Boaz). Ruth and Boaz's Union brought peace of mind and source of pleasure to the life of Ruth and Naomi. The interesting part of this friendship is that, out of this friendship, came out Jesse. Jesse gave birth to David, and from David were twenty-eight generations according to the record of Matthew:

> *"So all the generations from Abraham to David are fourteen generations, and from David until the carrying away into Babylon is fourteen generations, and from the*

> *carrying away into Babylon unto Christ are*
> *fourteen generations."*

*[Matthew 1King 1:17, KJV]*

I appreciate this story so much that I love telling the story anywhere because it portrays the reward of a devoted and a sincere friend. It is very delightful to know that our Lord savior came out of the lineage of Ruth. Imagine if Ruth had not followed Naomi back to her people, maybe she would have not enjoyed a peace of mind at the end, or maybe she wouldn't be anywhere in the history or lineage of Jesus Christ. Most time not all that sparkle can be regarded as gold and not all gold will shine brightly even with flashes of light, most especially in their crude form. It's always advisable to seek God's guidance to know who to be committed to as we have seen in the case of Ruth and Naomi so that we will not miss that which is destined for us.

## What is the Bible standpoint on Friendship?

One will ask questions like "what exactly is the Bible perspective on friendship" the bible is known to be a living manual for every Christian, but does scriptures actually tell us how we ought to choose our friends? Or where can we find references for friendship in the Holy Book? How can we be a true friend to others? And lastly, how do we express love to one another, if we have to do it in the ways that please God? It is a good thing to be curious about questions like this. I will like to let you know that all of those are vital issues that demand you to research the Bible, so as to be able to answer them in spirit and in truth. I will like to leave you with the verses below, so as to satisfy your curiosity. I am so sure that these great Bible Verses will do the speaking, and enhance your understanding of the prominent subject of friendship.

## FRIENDSHIP ACCORDING TO OUR SAVIOR

> *"This is My commandment that you love and unselfishly seek the best for one another, just as I have loved you. No one has greater love [nor stronger commitment] than to lay down his own life for his friends. You are my friends if you keep on doing what I command you. I do not call you servants any longer, for the servant does not know what his master is doing; but I have called you [My] friends because I have revealed to you everything that I have heard from My Father."*
>
> *[John 15:12-15, AMP]*

> *"And I tell you [learn from this], make friends for yourselves [for eternity] using the wealth of unrighteousness [that is, use material resources as a way to further the work of God], so that when it runs out, they will welcome you into the eternal dwellings."*
>
> *[Luke 16:9 AMP]*

## FRIENDSHIP ACCORDING TO THE WORDS OF WISDOM

"Make no friendship with an angry man; and with a furious man thou shalt not go."

(Proverbs 22:24)

"A friend loves at all times, and a brother is born for adversity."

(Proverbs 17:17)

"He who loves the purity of heart and whose speech is gracious will have the king as his friend."

(Proverbs 22:11)

"Faithful are the wounds of a friend [who corrects out of love and concern], But the kisses of an enemy are deceitful [because they serve his hidden agenda]."

(Proverbs 27:6)

"But there is a [true, loving] friend who [is reliable and] sticks closer than a brother."

(Proverbs 18:24, AMP)

"Do not abandon your own friend and your father's friend, and do not go to your brother's house on the day of your disaster. Better is a neighbor who is near than a brother who is far away."

(Proverbs 27:10)

"Whoever walks with the wise becomes wise,
but the companion of fools will suffer harm."

(Proverbs 13:20)

"The man of too many friends [chosen
indiscriminately] will be broken in pieces and
come to ruin."

(Proverbs 18:24)

"Oil and perfume make the heart glad; So does
the sweetness of a friend's counsel that comes
from the heart."

(Proverbs 27:9)

"Many will seek the favor of a generous and
noble man, and everyone is a friend to him
who gives gifts."

(Proverbs 19:6)

## DISEASE FROM THESE, IF YOU MUST BE A TRUE FRIEND

"Ye adulterers and adulteresses, know ye not
that the friendship of the world is enmity with
God? whosoever, therefore, will be a friend of
the world is the enemy of God."

[James 4:4]

"A perverse man spreads strife and one who
gossips separates, intimate friends."

[Proverbs 16:28]

"He who covers and forgives an offense seeks love, but he who repeats or gossips about a matter separates, intimate friends."

[Proverbs 17:9]

## YOU CAN BE A TRUE FRIEND

"If you sell anything to your friend or buy from your friend, you shall not wrong one another."

[Leviticus 25:14]

"For the despairing man there should be kindness from his friend; So that he does not abandon (turn away from) the fear of the Almighty."

[Job 6:14 AM]

"[God Restores Job's Fortunes] The Lord restored the fortunes of Job when he prayed for his friends, and the Lord gave Job twice as much as he had before."

[Job 42:10 AMP]

# PONDER POINTS

......................................................

*Stop trying to change others in the manner you wish,*
*since even you cannot fashion yourself in the manner you*
*wish because only God can alter the heart of a man.*

*Creatively visualize yourself as a winner, as that will*
*unfathomably contribute to your success. Remember*
*celebrated living always start with that creative*
*visualization, held in your imagination, of your aspiration.*

# CHAPTER THREE

# Four Steps to Choosing the Right Friends

## LOVE YOURSELF

You have to love yourself before you can even think of loving somebody else. And if you love yourself, you must care for anything that has to do with yourself, your future. You have to also feel good about yourself as this will reveal how much love you've got for yourself. It is of great necessity to realize that when you feel so good about yourself, you will allure, excel and evince the excitement of your being even better. You have to egoistically seek your own inner joy as this is the most substantial gift you can furnish anyone with, because unless one is full of this unspeakable joy, one will have got nothing to give as it is practically impossible to give out what you don't have. The scripture says "love your neighbor as you love yourself" this means you must love yourself first if you must obey this command of God and fulfill his purpose for your life, first thing first, value yourself as you want to be valued in life. The knowledge you have about yourself will significantly influence how you value yourself.

> As David, the psalmist, put it, *"I will praise thee, for I am fearfully and wonderfully made, marvelous are thy works (in my life) and that my soul knoweth right well."*
>
> *[Psalm 139:14]*

This scripture helps you understand that you are not an ordinary person; you were wonderfully created. You have to always appreciate God for His incredible artistry and for making you who you are today.

Here is another scripture describing you.

> *"But ye are a chosen generation, a royal*
> *priesthood, a holy nation, a peculiar people;*
> *that ye should shew forth the praises of him*
> *who hath called you out of darkness into his*
> *marvelous light."*

> *[1 Peter 2:9]*

I am certain that when you have a better perception of who you are (of God), you will have no other option than to love yourself. The second greatest commandment in the Bible is the one of love. Appreciate God for creating you by loving yourself as a beautiful creature. Make Him happy for creating you in His own image by taking good care of yourself. Your expectations in life depend on lots of things but mostly on you. You may succeed if nobody else believes in you, but you will never succeed nor forgive yourself if you don't believe in yourself. You will need to change the picture you have of yourself because when the image is changed, it will bring a dramatic change to your performance; and whatsoever is attached to these words "I am," that you will become. In other words, I believe that you should "Creatively visualize yourself as a winner, as that will unfathomably contribute to your success. Remember, celebrated living always start with that creative visualization, held in your imagination, of your aspiration."

## EXAMINE YOURSELF

For you to have the right friends, you will need to examine yourself. What are the qualities you wouldn't want to see in a friend and are you sure you are not guilty of those very things? Let us not deceive ourselves here. As regard the above statement, the Bible urges us to

> *"Examine yourselves, whether ye be in the faith; prove your own selves. Know ye not your own selves, how that Jesus Christ is in you, except ye be reprobates?"*

> *[11 Corinthians 13:5]*

You will need to choreograph yourself and do those things you would like to see in another person; behave the way you would like to see others act. Then the right friends can be attracted to you.

Remember what the law of attraction says: like attracts like. My point here is that;

"If positivity is the rudiment of your attitude when anticipating and envisaging enjoyment, gratification, and happiness, you will allure and build people, create situations and promotes events which uphold your unequivocal expectations."

According to The laws of attraction, you attracted the people in your life today as a result of your lifestyle, your character, and your habits. And this has gone a long way to explaining that being compulsively eye-catching is about living a life that feels splendid to you. It's a complete transformation from the inside. You will mostly attract most things in a tip-top condition when you feel so delightful about yourself, and it will be easy to set up circumstances in your life that work loveliest for you. In other words, you don't only attract those things that you are optimistic or wish for yourself; and also attract the people and environments that match how you're operating and showing up in the world. Most of us vigorously chase after those things we desire and some of us just naturally attract that which we actually want. It is natural that when we start living a life that feels most appealing to us, we start becoming more like the things we want to attract. For example, if you want to experience happiness, be happy. If kindness is what you desire from people, then be kind first. If you want more honor from others, give honor to people. As regard this subject, let me tell you how I view this world;

"The world is like a magnificent mirror that reflects back to you the exact picture of who you are. If you think you are loving, friendly and helpful, the world will reflect love, friendship, and help in return, and if you are full of hatred, wickedness, and evil, guess what, this mirror will reflect hatred, wickedness, and evil in like manner."

Your world is a reflection of who you are and what you give. If you change your way of living today, expect to see a change in the type of friends you will be attracting. For you to attract the right friends in your life, you must be ready to make a total change to your old ways and repent of your old lifestyle. After repenting of your old ways here is the good news for you.

> *"Therefore if any man [be] in Christ, [he is]*
> *a new creature: old things are passed away;*
> *behold all things become new."*

> *[11 Corinthians 5:17]*

All things, including your friends, will become new. This may not happen automatically, as you may have to work it out by making some drastic decisions as regards your new life in Christ.

If you are not thinking of changing your life pattern for a better one, then you shouldn't even think of helping to change another person's, because a blind man cannot lead a blind man in the right direction. However, if you are ready to make a new beginning in your life today, I would like to assure you that Christ has been waiting for this opportunity to turn your life around and to help you experience a new and fulfilled life.

Since you have been reading and (hopefully) examining yourself at the same time, we have been able to see that all Christ needs to help us live right is the opportunity to prove himself in our life. As we proceed to the next step, we will get a clearer image of why we need the help of Christ in our friendship.

## ACKNOWLEDGE GOD

> *"Lean on, trust in, and be confident in the Lord with all your heart and mind and do not rely on your own insight or understanding. In all your ways know, recognize, and acknowledge Him, and He will direct and make straight and plain your paths."*
>
> *[Proverbs 3:5-6] AMP*

God wants to always play a role in every situation you find yourself. What role do you think God always loves to play? It is a function of direction. He will never hesitate to direct your path if you play your own role of acknowledging Him. God desires us to always place Him first in all that we do because there is nothing you can actually do in this life that will be successful without God. You must be acquainted with His ways and direction that you will always be a beneficiary of His wisdom and guidance (Indeed, you will appreciate life so much more when you do anything under His leading). As you continue to read through this chapter you will discover even more that Jesus Christ is the only perfect friend; He is the only one who can guide us through the journey of life. He also knows the heart of everyone. Unless you are deceiving yourself, you cannot know what is going on in the heart of another person no matter how long you've known each other.

> *"The heart of a man is deceitful above all things and desperately wicked: who can know it? I the Lord search the heart, I try the reins even to give every man according to his ways, and according to the fruit of his doings."*

> *[Jeremiah 17:9-10]*

This part of the scripture helps us understand that He knows the heart of everyone. He will always lead you in the right direction. No wonder the psalmist said,

> *"He leadeth me in the path of righteousness for his namesake."*

> *[Psalm 23:3]*

God promises us that if we live depending on Him each day, He will make sure that we are always on course. He will give his approval as he deems fit, to preserve all our footsteps. That's why it was said in one of his proverbs, that we should commit our work unto him and our thoughts will be established.

This was David's prayer,

*"Lead me, oh Lord, in your righteousness because of my enemies, make your way straight before my face." [Psalm 5:8]* David prayed this prayer because he was convinced that God was able to show him what to do, and that is why he would always consult God before taking any step in his life.

## DO WE REALLY NEED TO INVOLVE HIM IN EVERYTHING WE DO?

Too often we may foolishly think we are competent enough to make wise choices without involving God. We reason, "If God gave us a brain, why is it so important to ask him for help or directions in making our decisions?" The answer becomes so apparent as we understand who God is, and how and why He invented us. He is knowledgeable about us better than we do. Life will be better for us if we can fully acknowledge God, just as David has shown us in this part of the scripture [Psalm 139:1-16]. It will gladden my heart to see you meditate on this, and put yourself in place of David and make this prayer with a genuine heart. You have searched me thoroughly, LORD, and you have known everything about me. You are aware of when I sit and when I rise up; you observe every of my thoughts from a distance. You detect my path, going out and my lying down; you are aware of all my ways. Even though my word is still unuttered, LORD, you understand it completely. You surrounded me in every angle of life, and you have laid your hand upon me. Such infinite knowledge is too magnificent for me, too giant for me to accomplish. Where can I ever go from your Spirit? Where can I ever flee to from your presence? If I reach up to the heavens, you are there; even if I make my bed in the depths, you are always there. If I upsurge on the wings of the sunrise, dwell on the far side of the sea, even there your hand will direct me, and your right hand will hold me. If I say, "Surely the darkness will shroud me, and the light become dark around me," even the darkness will never be dark to you; the night will shine to you like the day as darkness is as a shining light to you. For you did form my inmost being; you knit me together in my mother's womb. I will forever confess your praise because you have fearfully and wonderfully made me; your works are so beautiful; I know that right well. My frame was not a secret to you when I was made in the secret place when I was knit together in the depths of the earth. Your eyes saw my body when it was without a definite shape; all the days you predestined for me were penned in your book even before one of them came into existence. How precious to me are your thoughts, oh God? How vast is the sum of them? Only if I Were to count them, they would surely be more numerous than the sand of the sea when I awake, I could count till eternity I would still be with you. God, if only you, would eliminate the wicked away from me, and those who are bloodthirsty, they speak of you with wickedness in their heart; your enemies misuse your name. Do I not hate those that hate you, LORD, and detest those who are in defiance of you? I have nothing but absolute hatred for them; I count them, my enemies. Search me, God, and know my heart; try me and know my impatient thoughts. See if there is any wicked and offensive way in me, and lead me in the way everlasting.

God is in control of everything that happens. He is all mighty God:

> *"Ah, Sovereign LORD, you have made the heavens and the earth by your great power and outstretched arm. Nothing is too hard for you."*

> *[Jeremiah 32:1]*

He rewards each person according to their conduct and as their deeds deserve. He desires the best for us. That was why he gave His only begotten Son to us as the perfect friend who can help us with real friends that can be an instrument to our uplifting.

He who did not spare his own Son, but gave him up for us all—how will he not also, along with him, graciously give us all things? [Romans 8:32]

Remember, what the scripture says in Romans 1:18-32 - God will judge those who think they do not need Him in their decision making.


## BE FRIENDLY AND LOVELY

The scripture states that *"A man that hath friends must show himself friendly" [Proverb 18:24]*. It is paramount that you be friendly if you wish to make and keep real friends. Being friendly means behaving towards someone in a way that shows that you love them and are ready to listen to them, talk to them and also help them. A friend in need is a friend indeed, not only when there is a financial need, but also in other aspects of life. You have to be there for them always, whenever they need you. You have to show love to them. Remember also the proverb that said a friend loves at all time.

> *"Follow peace with all men, and holiness, without which no man shall see the Lord."*
>
> *[Hebrew 12: 14]*

Make yourself a Christ-like example; let your lifestyle preach the gospel of Christ without talking much. In friendship, actions speak louder than words. Make sure that your communication is always of grace and seasoned with salt, so that not only will your response be uplifting and edifying, but it will also be delivered in a pleasant way.

In the subsequent chapter, we will look at this topic in greater depth; you will discover that being friendly and lovely are major factors of becoming a good leader.

> **"Being a true friend to others will pave the way for Excellence in leadership."**

# PONDER POINTS

..............................................................

*That person you have chosen to be your closest friend
or included in your circle of friends today is one of the
most essential resolutions you will ever be opportune
to make during the journey of your life and destiny.*

*A long time ago, I decided that I will never continue a
friendship of any kind or even a mere chat without relating
it to the potentials which both propel and navigate my life.*

# CHAPTER FOUR

# Choose the Right Friends Now

> *"Blessed is the man that walketh not in the counsel of the ungodly, nor standeth in the way of sinners, nor sitteth in the seat of the scornful. But his delight is in the law of the LORD, and in his law doth, he meditates day and night.*
>
> *And he shall be like a tree planted by the rivers of water, that bringeth forth his fruit in his season; his leaf also shall not wither, and whatsoever he doeth shall prosper."*
>
> *[Psalm 1:1-3]*

The quintessential advantage to your future is that you can still choose; you can still decide. Why not make the decision today? Remember your decisions determine your destiny. At one point in my life, I discovered that every successful person I've ever gotten an encounter with had a crossroad. The crossroad was when they made a clear, distinct, and determined unequivocal decision that they were not going to continue to live like this anymore; they took a decisive action to achieve success. Some people make that decision at the teenage years, and some people make it at adulthood, some at old age and most never make it all. Every great leap forward in your life comes after you have made a clear, distinct and indubitable decision of some kind.

If you don't decide what is important in your life, someone else will decide for you. A wise person makes his own decisions; an ignorant or fool follows public opinion. If you don't see the necessity, then don't worry about not making a decision; someone else will make it for you, whether you like it or not.

Do you know that your destiny is not a matter of chance? It is a matter of choices placed before you. You shouldn't be found in the middle of the road, as that is a very dangerous place to be. You can get bashed by upcoming traffic from both directions, in other words, stop playing the game, stop trying and just make that decision. Listen to yourself carefully, if you are saying "I have decided," then you are on a path towards an exciting and productive life. Remember your decision determines your destiny. Remember chapter one ponder point,

> **"You will continue to be the same person, and will remain in the same place for years to come except for these two most important things, your circle of friends and your sources of information."**

Avoid negative people at all cost. These are the ones that I fear so much because they are the greatest destroyers of self-confidence and self-esteem. The less you associate with some of these people, the more you will improve in life. Hear what this proverb says: *"Putting confidence in an unreliable man is like chewing with a sore tooth, trying to run with a broken foot."* [*Proverb 25:19*]

Your true friends are those who bring out the best in you. You should be better, not worse after you've been around them. Most times a single conversation with the right person can be more valuable than many years of study in life, and so likewise evil communication can be more destructive just as it was seen in the case of Eve and the serpent. If you will look back to the departure of Adam and Eve from the Garden of Eden, a land of abundance, started with an evil communication with the serpent. Just before you choose that friend, it will be paramount to first investigate your options thoroughly. Remember *"the way that seems right unto a man may be the way that leads to destruction." [Proverb 14:12]*

The serpent may be a flake that's coming towards you, pretentious to be friendly, similar to the one in the garden but you may not notice it.

Don't always make decisions by the leading of your first impression. It does not necessarily give you an accurate picture. You may want to ask; why should I be the one to choose my friends? Some will say, "I am a free man, I meet different people every day, so everybody is my friend, I am very social I like everybody, nobody is my friend" and so much more. You may even support your opinion with the scriptures. We often say such things without accessing out options, without considering the characters and lifestyle involved, because we are ignorant of who we are and, even more, of the blessings and curses involved in friendship. We even go as far as describing people we don't know very well as friends. When I say people you don't know very well I mean you have not actually studied or got to know them to see if they are harmful or not; you don't even know if they will appreciate you or depreciate you, bless you or curse you. Let me briefly show you in the scripture, the blessings of finding yourself the right companions.

Blessed (happy, fortunate, prosperous, and enviable) is the man who walks and lives not in the counsel of the ungodly [following their advice, their plans and purposes], nor stands [submissive and inactive] in the path where sinners walk, nor sits down [to relax and rest] where the scornful [and the mockers] gather.

But his delight and desire are in the law of the Lord, and on His law (the precepts, the instructions, the teachings of God) he habitually meditates (ponders and studies) by day and by night.

And he shall be like a tree firmly planted [and tended] by the streams of water, ready to bring forth its fruit in its season; its leaf also shall not fade or wither, and everything he does shall prosper [and come to maturity].

Not so the wicked [those disobedient and living without God are not so]. But they are like the chaff [worthless, dead, without substance] which the wind drives away.

Therefore the wicked [those disobedient and living without God] shall not stand [justified] in the judgment, nor sinners in the congregation of the righteous [those who are upright and in right standing with God].

> "For the Lord knows and is fully acquainted
> with the way of the righteous, but the way of
> the ungodly [those living outside God's will]
> shall perish (end in ruin and come to naught)."

> Psalm 1:6 AMP]

You had better be wise in making or choosing the right friends now before it is too late or before you end up in ruin. Though people may condemn you for being reserved, and for segregating yourself, it's worth it, because of what you have inside of you and because of where God is taking or leading you to. As children of God, we should always make sure we take the time to choose the right friends in other to please God, as it is shown in the

Bible, as a primary condition of His blessings. The great people we admire today chose their friends. In many cases, their friends were considered greater or more important than they at the initial stage of the journey, but often, before the mid-stage of that voyage, they became grander than their friends. That was only possible because they kept their focus on their prospect, on their vision of the future. When you choose great friends, you will always thirst for greatness. The desire, passion, and drive for greatness will begin to propel you forward to greatness.

**NOTE:** Greatness is not just about finance or material things. Rather, greatness is about what you have inside of you and the ability and drive to be a solution to your generation. The technology you enjoy today is as a result of the kind of decisions the great men have made. Whenever you refuse to acknowledge the kind of people that come into your life, you open the doors of your life, allowing enemies often uncontrollable access, thus messing up your life. Trust me, if you choose the right friends, then you decide greatness.

People will always respect or disrespect you when they see the kind of friends you hang out with. Remember that you are the light of the world; you have no relationship with darkness or strange people. If you think you are a ray of light, why not choose another ray of light so that you can shine forth as a beam of light. Choose the Jesus kind of friends, friends that are always concerned with the things of the kingdom of God. With such friends, you can always edify each other with the word of God, pray together, and share ideas without fear or threat. These friends have goals, a drive for greatness, right character, and acknowledge their purpose on earth.

Sadly, if you refuse to choose the right friends now, it means that you are heading for doom or destruction. Among the people you come across every day, you must make choices. It's not enough to lay out your options; you must also consider the probable result of each action or decision you make. If the problem is an approaching shark like the enemy, then considering the consequence of each alternative, like choosing the right friends, and listing options, can be very helpful.

For example, if selecting a particular friend means having to desert your family, harboring ungodly relationships, committing sin, disobedience, gossiping, backsliding as a believer, domestic violence, sexual atrocities, then choosing that particular friend could lead to many adverse changes in habits. Some of these are immoral behaviors, failure, lackadaisical attitude, and behavioral disorder, wickedness, jail time, bad record and so on. All these may be a significant reason to choose another friend because that particular friend will destroy you. And don't forget to consider the steps in chapter three as well as the spiritual impact your decisions will have on you, your vision, your destiny and those around you including your families.

As a student then in the college, I knew that I was not very vast academically because of my lackadaisical attitude to study and poor study habits but what helped me then was that I made friends with the best students in the class. I hung out with them until I became academically balanced; but I did not just leave them hanging, I also helped them to achieve most things they couldn't have. You see, God used the friends I chose to deliver me from failure; and today I can continue to succeed wherever I find myself and no matter what I do. I always look for the person who knows better than I so that I can gain from them. In other words, I always endeavor to be in the circle of achievers.

Before you choose someone as a friend, make sure you have proper knowledge of that person. Just take your time and imagine the kind of people that person may be keeping as friends. Think of great people like **Bishop Thomas Dexter Jakes, Jr.**, chief Pastor of The Potter's House Church, Dallas Texas, **President Barack Hussein Obama II** the 44th and current President of the United States, and the first African-American to hold the office. **Bishop David O. Oyedepo** is a Nigerian Christian author, preacher, the founder and Presiding Bishop of Living Faith Church World Wide, also known as Winners' Chapel, **William Franklin "Billy" Graham, Jr**. An American Evangelical Christian evangelist, who was ordained as a Southern Baptist minister. He who rose to being in the limelight in 1949 reaching a core constituency of middle-class, moderately conservative Protestants, as of 2008, Graham's estimated lifetime audience, including radio and television broadcasts, topped 2.2 billion. **William Henry "Bill" Gates III** is a well-known American business tycoon, philanthropist, inventor investor and computer programmer,. Steven **Paul "Steve" Jobs** was an American entrepreneur, marketer, and inventor, who was the co-founder, chairman, and CEO of Apple Inc. **Warren Edward Buffett** is a distinguished American business tycoon, investor, and humanitarian. He was the most wealthy investor of the twentieth century. Presently the CEO, chairman, and leading shareholder of Berkshire Hathaway, and time after time ranked among the world's richest people. He was rated as the world's richest person in 2008. Buffett was also the third wealthiest in 2011, in 2012 Time named Buffett one of the world's most influential people. **Mark Elliot Zuckerberg** an American computer programmer and Internet entrepreneur. He is the current chairman and C.E.O of Facebook Inc. He is most recognized among the five founders of Facebook. As of 2013, Zuckerberg is the current Chairman C.E.O of Facebook Inc. and his worth, as of July 2014, is estimated to be $33.1 billion and so many other great men that are not mentioned here. Do you think these achievers above would have friends that would mess up their destiny or future? No, they all have great friends that were once higher or better than they were in one way or the other. The good thing about life is that, if you are willing to learn what the most flourishing people did in any area and then you did the same thing over and over, you'd eventually get the same result they got. The greatness of a man is a product of his companions.

When you approach people, go by what is of interest to you, for example, if you are called into ministry, then look for greater people already in ministry or people of like mind, that you can choose as friends. This was clearly demonstrated by David and Jonathan in chapter eighteen of 1Samuel. My heartfelt prayer for you is that God will always furnish you with the wisdom to operate in life and that He will always guide your paths. The reality of life is that your love and passion for a particular activity, job, hobby, talents, gift, or the game goes a long way in choosing the right friend. It is one that is equal, knows better or is mature in how they think and operate. When you make friends with great men or those that are like minded in vision or action, often with time, you will become great as well. You will see yourself sitting and dining with great men earlier in your life than you could ever imagine. Keep away from negative people who will trivialize your ambition. Small people always do that; the really great people make you feel that you, too, can become great. You will be wide-open to many areas of life, and you will also be connected to a network of great men, giving you access to places where even your possessions or your money cannot take you to at that moment. But let me encourage you with this: Don't ever underestimate yourself or feel overawed by any intimidating factor when you seem to be the lowest in any coterie of great men that you may find yourself. If you follow this book very well, you will discover that the difference between you and those great people is time. You may one day have to preside over their meetings. In other words, you may someday become a president in that robust network. There will be this point in time when people will consider you better or greater than they are. These people and those who consider you to be on the same level as they are will seek to make you their mentor, if only you can make that life changing decision by choosing great people as your friends now.

Most time when some great men discover that you are not harmful, you have something to offer to the world and are ready to learn, and you are drawing closer to them, they will bring you closer to them like a brother. And show you the way to greatness, but they only do this with people that are loyal, hardworking and honest. But if you choose lesser people, it may mean you only want to be disparaging in life, because you cannot be going to the top and still be strongly connected to the bottom of the ladder. They will create a drag to your flight. They will never allow you to soar to a greater height in life because some of them are comfortable at their current level and they wouldn't want to be alone or lonely in that overcrowded bottom of life's ladder. There are still others who will keep you down while they get as much as they can, from the little you have. Once they are contented with all that can be gotten from you, they then move ahead of you. Such people use you as their ladder to the top.

**NOTE:** The way you go about choosing your friends and the friends you choose will be mistaken for pride or arrogance by some, but sometime in the future, they will realize that they were wrong. By then you may be a role model or a mentor to some of them.

I also encourage you to develop your self-worth. This is a strong feeling of confidence in yourself, the belief that you are great, and the knowledge that you are powerful just like the scripture has stated below.

> *"I have strength for all things in Christ Who empowers me [I am ready for anything and equal to anything through Him Who infuses inner strength into me; I am self-sufficient in Christ's sufficiency."*

### [Philippians 4:13 AMP]

This comes from knowing who you are in Christ. The Bible tells us clearly how much God values and how you should value yourself.

> "I will praise You, for I am fearfully and wonderfully made; Marvelous are Your works)
> And that my soul knows very well."
>
> [Psalm 139:14]

"To whom God would make known what is the riches of the glory of this mystery among the Gentiles; which is Christ in you, the hope of glory."

[Colossians1:27]

"Ye are the salt of the earth: but if the salt has lost his savor, wherewith shall it be salted? It is thenceforth good for nothing, but to be cast out, and to be trodden under foot of men. Ye are the light of the world. A city that is set on a hill cannot be hidden."

[Matthew5:13-14]

"For as many as are led by the Spirit of God, they are the sons of God. For ye have not received the spirit of bondage again to fear; but ye have received the Spirit of adoption, whereby we cry, Abba, Father. The Spirit itself beareth witness with our spirit that we are the children of God: And if children, then heirs; heirs of God, and joint-heirs with Christ; if so be that we suffer with him, that we may also be glorified together."

[Romans 8:14-17]

"He who believes in Me [who cleaves to and trusts in and relies on Me] as the Scripture has said, from his innermost being shall flow [continuously] springs and rivers of living water."

[John 7:38 AMP]

You are identified with Christ and likewise Christ in you. How I wish you could understand this now, so you will know the right decision to make when choosing that friend. By now you should have started to consider and have perhaps discovered whether or not the friends you are keeping right now are worth it and whether they fit into the path of your destiny.

I plead with you today that you make the wise choice by selecting the right friends. It is better to do it now and bear all the pain and insult now, rather than feeling sorry when it is too late.

Also, make sure that when choosing a friend, that you are not being influenced by worldly things like money, material things or by fleshy desires, because if you allow yourself to be carried away with this stuff, you will create enmity with God. *"Know ye not that the friendship of the world is enmity with God? Whosoever, therefore, will be a friend of the world is the enemy of God" [James 4:4],* so be wise. Don't start making friends just because of their wealth or because of the little enjoyment that may later bring about a life of poverty or suffering. Don't allow yourself to be enticed with material things; you may not know when you will cheaply sell your birthright like Esau sold his to Jacob.

## CHOOSE THE COMPANY OF EAGLES NOW AND SOAR TO GREATER HEIGHTS IN LIFE

Just before you decide, do you know that love shows the character of a man?

A genuine character of a man is revealed by what he loves dearly. For as a man think in his heart, so is a man according to the content of his heart, so likewise for as a man love, so is the man according to his love, so you may confidently designate the person. If he is a lover of honor, then we can designate him to be an ambitious man; if a lover of pleasure, he can be identified as sensual; if primarily loves the world, then he is a greedy man. If a man basically loves righteousness, he may be a religious man; if he loves Christ and the things above with a preeminent love, he is a heavenly minded man, sincere and a faithful man of God.

Be selective about your external influences, because your brain is multi-dimensional and can easily be influenced by almost everything you see, hear, read, smell, touch, feel or say if not under any form of control. I strongly encourage you to get with the right people. I will also recommend you Associate with positive, goal-oriented individuals who encourage and inspire you, as that is the way that leads to greatness. Know this from now on that you are fully responsible for everything in your life and you will someday have to give a full account of it.

# PONDER POINTS

......................................................

*Almost the totality of your well-being will be determined
by the class of people you associate with at every phase
and area of your life. How well you concur with people,
how much they esteem and regard you, and how much
love they show you, has an extraordinary influence
on the caliber of your life than any other factor.*

*There are these four significant things that
lead to a more celebrated life: sharing, caring,
daring and the most of all loving always.*

# CHAPTER FIVE

# Four Elements of Relationship that Makes You A True Friend

I cannot talk about friendship without helping you become a true friend to others. You cannot be a true friend for others without being friendly and lovely. As the book of wisdom has made it clear that *"A man that has friends must show himself friendly, there is a friend that sticketh closer than a brother"* *[Proverb 18:24]*.

Being friendly, straightforwardly means behaving towards someone in a way that evinces your love for them, that indicates that you want to talk to them and demonstrate that you are always ready to listen to them. This also means that for you to be referred to as a true friend, you should always be friendly and lovely at all times. This doesn't say you should be perfect as nobody, but God is perfect. At the end of this chapter, you will discover that to be a true friend makes you a good leader. When you are friendly and lovely, you may be able to lead in any circle you find yourself because you have the primary characteristics of a good leader.

Let's take a look at the four (4) elements of being friendly; the same makes a true friend and a good leader.

**LOVE PEOPLE**

Christ made this clear when he said: *This is my commandment, that you love one another as I have loved you* [John 15:12]. He also went ahead to make us understand that: *If a man says, I love God and hates his brother, he is a liar: for he that loves not his brother whom he has seen, how can he love God whom he has not seen? [I John 4:20]*

Beloved, if God so loved us, we ought also to love one another (1John 4:11 – 21). Love is an act of unconditional forgiveness, a tenderhearted way of life which becomes a habit. It is by loving instead of being loved, as it is more blessed to give than to receive, that one can come closer to the soul of another. Being loved is the second preeminent thing in the world; loving someone is preeminent. Love sought-after is good but love established unsought is healthier. You must love them for you to be the right friend. Love people for who they are (their personality) not their color, race, or culture. Do you know that our willingness to open up about who we are encourages trust and openheartedness on the part of the other person? So be yourself, be real and genuine when showing love to people. Love is not a once in a while business, it is meant to be a continuous decisive action to live as God has commanded, like I said earlier, love should be a way of life. We have to do everything in love. It is an actual fact, that when we act in love, we can live very reliable, sensitive, tough and tenderhearted in friendship, relationship, family, as well as in our day-to-day life. When we submit ourselves to Christ out of sincere love for Him, we find an indubitable power to love and effectuate all things as scriptures have assured us that we can do all things through Christ who strengthens us. In our world today, nobody cares how much you know until they see how much you care. God made this very clear and comprehensible to us when he said:

> *"And thou shall love the Lord thy God with all thy heart, and with all thy soul and with all thy might and with all thy strength. This is the first commandment, and the second is like namely this, thou shall love thy*

> *neighbors as thyself. There is none another*
> *commandment greater than these."*
>
> *[Mark 12:30-31]*

From the Word of God (logos) as you have read, love is the greatest commandment in life. If you must please God, you must love people without reservation, just as you have loved yourself. In the book of John Christ maintains that:

> *"A new commandment I give unto you, that*
> *ye love one another; as I have loved you, that*
> *ye also love one another. By this shall all*
> *men know that you are disciples if ye have*
> *love one to another."*
>
> *[John 13:34-45]*

When you show love to people, it preaches the gospel of Christ; as they say "action speaks louder than voice." For you to prove your identity in Christ, you must love others as you love yourself. I can hear you asking yourself, where do I start from? Don't stress it, but remember we learn to walk by walking, to run by running, to fly by flying, to work by working, and, in the same manner, you get to love people by loving. The journey of a thousand mile always start with the first mile, so start loving from this moment and make it a habit. The essence of love was greatly emphasized by Apostle Paul; he wrote this letter to correct the specious notions in the Corinthian church at that time. In his writings, he wrote about the excellence and the beauty of love. I love the way the Amplified version of the Bible made it straightforward and understandable, that even a little kid will understand the excellence of love. According to Paul "If I articulate with the tongues of men and of angels, but have not love [for others growing out of God's love for me], then I have become only a noisy gong or a clanging cymbal [just an annoying distraction]. And if I have the gift of prophecy [and speak a new message from God to the people]. And understand all mysteries, and [possess] all knowledge; and if I have all [sufficient] faith so that I can remove mountains, but do not have love to reaching out to others], I am nothing. If I give all my possessions to feed the poor, and if I surrender my body to be burned, but do not have love, it does me no good at all. Love endures with patience and serenity, love is kind and thoughtful, and is not jealous or envious; love does not brag and is not proud or arrogant. It is not rude; it is not self-seeking, it is not provoked [nor overly sensitive and easily angered]; it does not take into account a wrong endured. It does not rejoice at injustice, but rejoices with the truth [when right and truth prevail]. Love bears all things [regardless of what comes], believes all things [looking for the best in each one], hopes all things [remaining steadfast during difficult times], endures all things [without weakening]. Love never fails [it never fades nor ends]. But as for prophecies, they will pass away; as for tongues, they will cease; as for the gift of special knowledge, it will pass away. For we know in part, and we prophesy in part [for our knowledge is fragmentary and incomplete]. And now there remain faith [abiding trust in God and His promises], hope [confident expectation of eternal salvation], love [unselfish love for others growing out of God's love]. These three [the choicest graces]; but the greatest of these is love (1 Corinthians 13 AMP). With all that been said, how can you be a true friend without loving? It is scripturally impossible.

## LISTEN TO THEM

Listening can be defined as the potential to precisely accumulate and elucidate messages in the communication process. It is a very paramount core in communication if it must be considered effective. Without this potential, communication could easily be misapprehended, leaving the conveyor of the message frustrated. Excellent listening skills can lead to a better satisfaction in communication, increased productivity and longevity with fewer mistakes in relationships and increases sharing of information that can lead to a more healthy and happy friendship. It has been carefully observed that most prosperous leaders and entrepreneurs ascribe their success to sensitive and efficient listening ability. It can also be viewed as a technique that supports all real, healthy and lasting friendship. It will be of great worth to spend some of your time working and developing your listening ability as it is the foundation or building block of a happy lifestyle.

Active listening skills also benefit us in various part of our personal lives. Most of our friends and affiliates have seen improvement in self-worth and self-assurance, and excellence in academic work or even improved health and well-being in general as a result of effective listening. Listening is quite different from Hearing. As hearing alludes to the sounds that you hear, listening tends to entail more than that: it demands focus. This means paying attention to details, not only to the tale but how it is told and expressed, the use of both body gesture, language and voice. In other words, it also means awareness of both verbal and non-verbal messages. Your capability to listen effectively significantly depends on the extent to which you discern and comprehend these messages.

The most fundamental and efficient way to connect with others is to listen. All they may ever need from you is to just be quiet and listen, as this is one of the most valuable things we can freely give each other.

Sensitive listening demands more concentration and employing the proper use of other senses, and not just hearing the spoken words alone, in other words, it is not the same as hearing. And to listen sensitively and more efficiently, you need to involve more than just your ears.

An effective listener will not only listen to what is being verbally conveyed but also to what is left unvoiced. Effective listening involves observing body languages and discerning inconsistencies and self-contradiction between verbal and non-verbal messages. For instance, if friends are telling you that they are happy with how everything is going on in their life but through body gestures like tears running down their cheek or negative facial expressions. You should be able to consider that the verbal and non-verbal messages are in dissension, it may just be that they don't mean what they say or they are just trying to be positive.

Sensitive listening and hearing is an open gold mine to friendship. In reality, the likelihood for listening before we talk has not yet being utilized, and it lolls within us like a shipload of unmined treasure. It is quite understood that every one of us has barriers that impede our listening to someone, some may be simple, and others may be complex in nature but remember that one way to show that you love them is by communicating acceptance to them. Many times we find ourselves doing more of the talking and less listening, and at the end of the conversation, we end up suggesting or recommending a solution without even being patient enough to listen to what the person is trying to relate to us. These always result in argument and frustration. Patiently listening to friends in love is one way of expressing such acceptance. An example, in this case, is the life of Jesus Christ, our perfect friend, whom we look up to. He is always expeditious to listen to us whether we are right or wrong. Most times, care and affection can be evidenced of how much we listen to people.

Listening is a creative force, and it is highly magnetic in nature as it has been observed that the friends who listen to us are the friends we incline to; we always want to be in the radius of those friends. When we are listened to, it recreates our mindset and give fresh vitality to the faith of a possible solution, it makes us unfold and expand in various aspect of life. You may ask what will I say after listening, remember that Christ is in you, and you in Christ and Christ in you is the hope of glory (Colossians 1:27). The Holy Spirit will always guide you as to what to say in every situation that comes to your attention. When people discover that you always listen to them sensitively and more efficiently with love, passion, and empathy and that you are willing to help them out, they will always want to be around you.

## TALK TO THEM

*"Let the word of Christ dwell in you richly in all wisdom, teaching, and admonishing one another in Psalms, hymns, and spiritual songs, singing with grace in your heart for the Lord." [Colossians 3:16].* As we have seen in this part of the scripture, we must be affluent in the word and the wisdom of

God to talk to friends in a Godly manner. To win and keep good friends, you must learn to speak regarding the other person's regard. The essential point you need to remember is this: to be of real help to your friends as they grapple with the issues of life, you must try and think yourself in their situations, encouraging, sympathizing and empathizing with them. It is not really helpful to espouse a "take it or leave it" attitude. You may find that you have to spend lots of time and trouble trying to explicate ideas and issues which are very obvious to you, but which your friends seem to have enormous difficulty in grasping. Always rely on God to help you whenever you find yourself in this kind of situation. You will also have to create time for them because it takes a lot of time to communicate, to work through conflicts and to build healthy relationships.

**NOTE:** In friendship, just as James 4:11 has said "Speak not evil one of another, brethren. He that speaketh evil of [his] brother, and judgeth his brother, speaketh evil of the law, and judgeth the law: but if thou judge the law, thou art not a doer of the law, but a judge". We are never supposed to speak of words that tear down our friends but instead, we are obliged to speak words that morally and spiritually elevates, inspiring happiness and moreover encouraging words that will cause a positive change in the life of our friends.

> *"Let your speech at all times be gracious (pleasant and winsome), seasoned [as it were] with salt, [so that you may never be at a loss] to know how you ought to answer anyone [who puts a question to you]."*
>
> *[Colossians 4:6]*

True friendship is a dedication to love, to fit into each other, to be acquainted with and apprehended, to care, to share, to dare, to sacrifices and out of that dedication, the action must follow, so talk to that situation of your friend today. I will encourage to never engage in any form of criticism, condemnation, gossiping and backbiting or diminish people because if you do so to those who you are called to love, help and serve then you've known nothing about the teaching or revelation of Christ. You must ask for the wisdom of God daily and also have a fear of God in you, as *"The fear of the Lord is the beginning of wisdom: and the knowledge of the holy is understanding" [Proverb 9:10].*

Always study the word of God so that words that come out of your mouth can have the power to influence a man to align himself with the will of God. And you cannot have this unless you subject yourself to the word of God. You cannot give what you don't have.

*"A good man out of the good treasure of his heart bringeth forth that which is good; and an evil man out of the evil treasure of his heart bringeth forth that which is evil: for of the abundance of the heart his mouth speaketh." [Luke 6:45].* So this verse of the scripture only put it to us that it is out of the abundance of the word of God in your heart that our mouth will speak out to people. The word of God in you is so powerful, but you may not know its power until you talk it out.

> *"For the word of God is living and active and full of power [making it operative, energizing, and effective]. It is sharper than any two-edged sword, penetrating as far as the division of the soul and spirit [the completeness of a person], and of*

*both joints and marrow [the deepest parts*
*of our nature], exposing and judging the*
*very thoughts and intentions of the heart.*
*And not a creature exists that is concealed*
*from His sight, but all things are open and*
*exposed, and revealed to the eyes of Him*
*with whom we have to give account."*

*[Hebrews 4:12AMP]*

Going by the above scripture, we can see that when the word of God's full in you, you can discern another man's thought and the intent of his heart. It is paramount to know that you can only consistently keep people's attention by focusing on what they value so much and the issues that are of a threat to their happiness. You may want to ask "how can I know that? The actual answer is that except the Lord build up a house the builders, they put together up in vain, except the Lord watch over a city, the watchmen will watch in vain, so likewise except the Lord speaks through you, your wise counsel will be turned to foolishness. Lastly, always make sure you explain to them with clarity because exhortation without clarification will undoubtedly lead to vexation.

**HELP THEM**

Friendship is some kind of feelings and thoughts, not out of trepidation or want, but out of a desire to be familiar with another's inner life and to be able to care, dare and share one's own burden. It is important to love others than they desire as God's desire is for you to be your brother's or sister's keeper, bearing one another's burden in love. I've discovered that prosperous people always have the quest for opportunities to help others while the vain people are always asking, 'what will be my gain.' Life's most untiring and dire questions are: 'what are you doing for others, what is your contribution towards helping others, what is your impact on this generation'? For you to be celebrated in life, you just have to help others to the top, consulting their weaknesses, relieving them of complaints, striving to uplift them and in doing so, you will most efficaciously uplift yourself as well. A friend in need is a friend without a doubt and a friend in indeed is a friend in need. They need your help as a friend. You should be concerned about them just as you are concerned about yourself. Treat them as you will treat God if God is physical with you. You can also help them by forgiving them in any way they might have offended you so badly because Christ said we should forgive. Lead them to Christ, introduce the eternal life (God's gift of love) to them. Make sure you are very interested in their spiritual and physical wellbeing. Help them with resources that will improve their lives. Don't be selfish to your friends; leave sentiment out of your daily dealings with people. Pray for your friends as your breakthrough may depend on it.

> *"And the Lord turned the captivity of job when he prayed for his friends."*

> *[Job 42:10].*

You can see how God turned the captivity of Job, just because he prayed for his buddies. God is always happy anytime you pray for your friends; you cannot pray for your friends and remain the same. You will always be celebrated all your life, only if you will help enough other people to be honored as well. Remember the ponder points, there are these four significant things that lead to a more illustrious life: sharing, caring, daring and the most of all loving always. Assign yourself the purpose of making others happy and fruitful. Your friends have a way of becoming what you encourage them to be.

If you are very sharp-eyed to what happens around you, it will be easy to decipher the two types of people in the world. Those who live for themselves (selfish) and those who live to help others, the first group are the vain people, while the second group is the flourishing ones. It pays to invest in other, help others like your life depends on it, it pays high dividends. Scripture has said, *"As we have therefore opportunity, let us do good unto all men, especially unto them who are of the household of faith." [Gal 6:10].*

In doing all these, you make yourself an excellent leader among your friends and beyond as these are the fundamental qualities of a good leader. A good leader is a leader that loves his people, listen to his people, talk to his people and help his people. This proves that, if you are worthy to be called a true friend, then you are also worthy of being a leader. No wonder Jesus Christ is a perfect friend and also an excellent head. We will dwell more on the perfect friend in the next chapter.

## RULES FOR DEVELOPING HEALTHY RELATIONSHIPS AND BECOME A BETTER FRIEND

### LET LOVE & TOLERATION BE YOUR WAY OF LIFE

You can show tolerance by respecting, accepting and appreciating the rich diversity of our world's cultures, customs, and traditions, our mode of articulation and ways of representing our uniquely human nature. Tolerance can also be viewed as a way of expression of thoughts and feelings, but most significantly, of action that gives us inner peace in our various distinction, reverence for those different from us, the wisdom to recognize human values and the valor to act upon them. Tolerance is simply agreement even in disparity. As you know quite well, we are all from a different demography, settings, environment, and culture. I know fully well, it's not that easy to understand someone who is not from the same background, but loving and tolerating people, regardless of where they come from or how they are made up gives you the possibility to develop a good relationship with those, others would never consider. I believe this world will be a lovelier place for you and me if only we can let love and tolerance be our guide.

## AVOID DISCRIMINATING, STEREOTYPING, AND PREJUDICE

> *"Judge not, that you be not judged. For with the judgment you pronounce you will be judged, and with the measure you use it will be measured to you."*
>
> *[Matthew 7:1-2]*

Discrimination is a behavior that treats people in an unjust manner. It is a prejudicial treatment given to different categories of individuals or things unequally because of their group, memberships or maybe their individual differences. Most discriminatory behaviors often begin with negative stereotypes and prejudices.

A stereotype is an extensively held but firm, false and oversimplified image or idea of a particular type of people, places or thing. It is a false belief that distorts the image or truth about a certain individual or group, a generalization that gives room for a wee or no individual differences or physical, social and spiritual variation. It can be positive or negative, but in most cases negative. It is mostly based on images projected by mass media, or character passed on by parents, friends and other members of society.

Prejudice is a preconceived opinion, prejudgment, attitude or idea about a group or its individual members that are not based on any genuine reason or real experience. Prejudice is not always negative, but in our usage in this book we are dealing with the negative attitude.

It usually co-occurs with ignorance, fear or hatred. It mostly initiated by a complex psychological process that started with attachment to a cohort of acquaintances or a coterie of family and friends. In most cases, prejudice is always aimed at out-groups or minorities.

The world we live in is heterogeneous in nature, you have to understand that the people you deal with every day are diverse, both in characters and the content of their heart. If you are sharp-eyed enough, you must have discovered that other people in your life, family members, your fellow students, colleagues, neighbors, and other people you interface with on a daily basis, look different. It maybe in height, symmetry, weight, physique, body, skin/hair color, mode of dressing, financial status, and language compared to you. We have some who may sound unlike us in their native dialect, accent, articulation, tone, vocal clarity, accent or not able to speak at all. And some who may be disparate in intellect, earning potential, athleticism, education, politics, social philosophies, sexual orientations, religion, beliefs, birth, brainpower, etc. For you to enjoy a happy and healthy relationship with people, these essential differences should be well respected as it will help us all get along well.

It is quite hapless that many of us were taught at an early age to judge others with uncomplimentary remarks if they are unlike us. For many of us, it all started when our parents or guardians were protecting us when they said to us "don't trust or talk to strangers." For some of us it was during grade school when we were told, "care about the homeless, but never walk near them because they can hurt, infect or kill you. And maybe finally by high school age, the sum of all the things we've been taught and heard from our parents, guardians, those involved in our upbringing and others we trusted. Our observation of real life, in movies and television, mass media and things we've experienced directly and indirectly through others' behaviors, actions and activities helped transmute these hostile way of life into prejudices. So, almost without realizing it, we have learned to stereotype an entire population of people based on the attitude and beliefs of just a few. It's quite unfortunate that we built some of our prejudices on a very solid foundation of falsehood and fear of the unknown. However, it has been seen that stereotyping in most cases has a negative effect and it is damaging to those who are stereotyped and also those who believe the stereotype are not left unaffected. As you strive daily for a happy and healthy relationships, you must forsake your prejudice, stereotype and discrimination out of your daily activities with people. Your potentials to become a better friend increase tremendously as you open your mind to the many differences you encounter and learn how they can be used to enhance peoples' quality of life.

## REHEARSE FRIENDLY GREETINGS

It always feels good to give a very nice first impression. For this reason, alone, you may need to sometimes stand in the front of your mirror and rehearse your first smile and greeting. You have to allow others recognize that you care and want to get to know more about them. For starters and those who are shy, try and work this out so that it may become real and a little easier for you.

## TRY REACHING OUT TO OTHERS

If you wait for others to reach out to you for a relationship or friendship, you may be waiting a very long time. We live in the days in which people are not willing or maybe scared to reach out in friendship, most of them have experienced painful relationships, and they don't seem to be in a hurry to get back into a relationship that makes them susceptible to others. If you are going to have a relationship with someone, realize that you will have to be one to initiate a relationship as this may help you select and choose your friends.

## GET OUT THERE AND MEET PEOPLE

Sitting at home like a loner or isolating yourself will not put you in a position to get that friend of your choice. Join a club, fellowship with people, volunteer in your church, school or community, participate in activities that physically involves other people, interact with people, etc. sometimes it's good to take walks with the objective to stop and talk to other people. I encourage you to get out there and meet people.

## HAVE MORE THAN ONE FRIEND

Most healthy and happy people have many connections, a few good friends, and two or three very close associates. It is precarious to have just one close friend. It is just too much of a Herculean task to have all your eggs in one basket or to put it all on only one friend. No single person should ever think of meeting that demand because no one person can carry all the virtue needed and remember as we are all unique in nature so also everybody has something unique to offer. It is inevitable that when you have more than one good friend, you will live a healthier life and you make a better friend, as two good heads are better than one.

## NEVER QUIT, GO THE SECOND MILE

If you quit on a friendship or relationship at the first disappointment, you will never have good friends, remember winners never quit, and quitters never win. Those you love most in life disappoint you more than anyone else. Always allow love and grace to operate in your relationship.

## THERE SHOULD BE A COMMON INTERESTS

Don't waste time accommodating the things that detach you from others, find consensus. Always look for something meaningful to get you communicating. Remember what I said earlier "Long time ago, I decided that I will never continue a friendship of any kind or even a mere chat without relating it to the potentials which both propel and navigate my life.'

## GIVE RECOGNITION AND ENCOURAGEMENT

Most people attach so much value to recognition, we all need someone to lift us up at various points in life. Learn to always recognize others achievement and let them know how important they are to you. This will enhance them with the opportunity for self-satisfaction and good feeling. It's paramount to know that it is not what you say to people but how you make them feel that is momentous.

## BE FLEXIBLE

They may not dress like you or want to eat in the same restaurants. Be flexible, you only love eating in fast food joints and your friends like eating the food they prepared themselves, one of you is going to have to be flexible if you are going to enjoy your relationship. The perfect example of someone who is a master of maintaining and creating perfect friendship is Jesus Christ. You will make an excellent friendship if you follow the example of the perfect friend and also learn to reach out to people out there.

## LET TRUTH AND HONESTY BE YOUR CORE VALUES

Honesty may seem to be like a slippery slope, it is practically more challenging than it sounds; but a weak friendship may not survive the test of truth and honesty. It must be the foundation of any relationship. Any friendship that is not based on reality will not last long. And that you are honest doesn't mean that you should be unkind, blunt or disrespectful, but just means sharing the truth in loving manner. Truth and honesty may hurt sometimes, but trust me only true friendship can survive and grow in the process. Let truth and honesty be the value of your relationships.

## LEARN TO BE RETICENT, BUT SUPPORTIVE

It is not uncommon to have a friend who is grappling in her marriage at some point or having difficulty with family members or another close friend. This may just be the time for you to be reserved because often times this relationship or family issues will be resolved; so if you are the one that says rude words about your friend's spouse, family members or friends, they will not be happily recollected by her. Even if you feel like buttressing her, be quiet for a while, all you may need to do is just listen. It is possible that she will try to get you to verbally belabor her spouse or family members, please for God's sake don't fall for it, but always make sure you are encouraging and supportive. If it is a case of an abusive relationship or threat to life, then some of these rules may not apply but let wisdom guide you always.

## FLEE FROM ALL APPEARANCE OF GOSSIP AND BACKBITING

Due to experience, I have been able to get closed to people who talk, tear down, destroy and run-down other people in their absence. Shortly after sometimes, I was able to figure it out this way; if they can tear other people down behind them to me, then it's plain and simple, same can be done to me in like manner. Avoid the mistake of believing that you are exempted from any form of gossip and backbiting; the same will be done to you. You may not necessarily need to talk about the scandal, but by little laughing and listening, you give your participation, and in so doing, you encourage the act. Never luxuriate in any form so that you won't have to fret about your malicious talk thrown back at you and also you won't have to regret and apologize for what you have said. I understand quite well that we all struggle in our relationships with others once in a while, but it is not a valid reason to tear someone down behind closed doors. Just imagine a situation where you've verbally destroyed somebody who regrettably ended up becoming your friend, if you've ever indulged in this kind of act, before getting close to that person, he or she will find out someday and may likely be hurt.

## DON'T BE TOO SENSITIVE

When you are excessively sensitive, you will think too much about yourself and your feelings about how everything goes in your relationship. If your close friends have to be extremely careful when they are in your radius, constantly fret much about hurting your feelings, then the friendship will experience a slow growth. Like I said previously, sincere and lasting friendship requires honesty, and it will be impracticable to be honest with you if you are overly sensitive.

There are times in our life when close friends amazingly address us in an unpleasant, irksome and vexatious manner; if you ever happen to find yourself in a situation like this, all you need to do is to bring to mind that the Bible warns us to be slow to anger. The Bible is only saying that you have to give yourself some time to think about it. And so as to make necessary and favorable considerations before reacting in order not to regret your actions; but if your feelings still remain hurt, you should first calm yourself down then discuss it, explaining why it hurt so bad. If that friend is a true friend, that may help clarify, correct and build your friendship further. You don't have to be scared of having to misunderstand them sometimes or live with the fear of making a mistake as it can help know each other better. Know it today that if you are too sensitive in any relationship, you will never get the best out of that friendship.

## DON'T GET YOURSELF IN THE MIDDLE

Friendships have their own daily struggle, ups, and downs. Relationships even get divided; if you are not careful, you could end up in the middle. Like I said earlier, be reserved but supportive, you should never allow yourself to come in between friends, marriages, families and associates. Always encourage them to work it out on their own. The danger of getting yourself in the middle is awful because, toward the end, it is very possible that they will both turn against you, so stop been nosy, get yourself out of other people's matter most especially when it doesn't concern you. Remember the bible says *"A perverse man sows strife, and a whisperer separates close friends" [Proverb 16:28AMP]*

## BE SACRIFICIAL

Most times real friendship demand giving up some of your desires occasionally. For example, if a friend gets married, maybe give birth, or may get a new demanding job, this may practically mean that you may not get as much time as you habitually get before the marriage, baby or that demanding job came. Know that this may not necessarily mean that your time with her is no more of the same quality as you are used to; it's just a difference in quantity. As a true friend that you are, you will have to make some unexpected sacrifices to maintain a healthy relationship. Rather than feeling downhearted, try to be understanding and gracious, and remember it could be you instead. Life is full of many changes, stages, and phases, as these are all ineluctable, true friendship has the ability to adjust to circumstances, adapt and grow through it all. If your friendship is not genuine, you may probably find it to be temporal during the test and trial of different times and weather.

## DON'T BE QUICK IN MAKING ASSUMPTIONS

Friends may really get busy sometimes, that may even dispossess them the time to call, chat, or maybe stay on the phone for a long conversation as usual and these are what we should be mindful of and understand carefully as situations may demand. It is of paramount importance to always let close friends know how your busy schedule may be so that they don't easily get aggrieved if you are unable to make that call or engage them in a normal lengthy conversation at that particular time.

Another assumption that I have noticed that frequently befall us in friendships is calling a friend, trying to engage in a long conversation that is not in order of importance, without fully acknowledging the state of the person's mind, situation and how busy your friend may be. In most cases, Assumptions gets us in serious trouble and always squash relationships. Please don't always believe what other people say about your friends without serious inquiries, they may just be jealous and envious of your healthy and happy relationship. Learn to eschew and pay no attention to them as they may be your haters, and haters don't always deserve your attention. The only attention they need is the one of Christ to change them.

Beloved, if you desire to be a better friend than you are right now, make these rules your guide and watch your relationships blossom. True friendship like any other relationship takes time and effort on both ends to make it work, and the reward is definitely worth the work.

# PONDER POINTS

......................................................

*No one has greater love [no one has shown stronger affection] than to lay down (give up) his own life for his friends.*
*(John 15:13) AMP*

*One compelling and fascinating thing about God's love is that you can never get enough of it, and there is nothing you can do to make it more or less, His love is unequaled, indubitable and unambiguous. It continues the same yesterday, today and forever more, even in the absence of your love.*

# CHAPTER SIX

# The Perfect Friend

His name is JESUS; let me tell you more about Him as this is what I have long been waiting for. Just before I go further, let me say what he's known for or what others call Him. There was a time when Jesus went on a journey with His disciples to the villages of Caesarea Philippi; and on their way, Jesus asked His disciples, who do men say that I am? I think at this point he wanted them to tell him who they think He was. He was keen to know how they see Him, also what they think of Him. And they answered Him and said, some call you John the Baptist, some others Elijah, some also believe that you are one of the prophets. Then He turned to His disciple and asked them, but who do you yourselves say that I am? At this time, he wanted to know directly what the disciples themselves called him or took him for, then Peter replied to Him, You are Christ the Messiah, the Anointed One. I can't even envision Jesus asking me that same question today; I will call him the author and the finisher of our faith, the bright and morning star, the omnipotent, omnipresent and omniscient God. The advocate, the lamb of God, the bread of life, the rose of Sharon, my mind regulator, the Holy One, the head of my family. I can go on and on, He is the All-Sufficient God.

The name Jesus as in New Testament Greek is "Iesosus" (e-ay-sees). You can find the origin of that name in the Old Testament name "Joshua, Jehoshuah or Jehoshaua" Pronounced Jehohushawa (ye-ho-shoo-ah) or Yehow shua. His name was not based on random choice or personal whim of any fashion but based upon his primary mission in life. And His mission was determined and concluded from the foundation of the world. Christ was to save us from our sins (Revelation 13:8) with one sacrifice that will last forever. The importance of the name of Jesus does not end with his noble mission in life. It was also found in writing and in action that Jesus is the only savior of mankind. The one true God, the only perfect friend who stretched out the heavens alone and spread the earth by himself (Isaiah 44:24). He came to earth to save us by all himself. God did not send someone else to save the world, he came himself.

In Jesus Christ, we find the greatest profundity of love, the ever-green portion of joy, the copious measure of peace. He is the initiator of love. Scriptures states:

> *"Greater love hath no man than this that a man lay down his life for his friends."*
>
> *[John 15:13]*

His love is permanent, wholehearted, unswerving, eager and genuine. His love never fails. He is that special friend that is always with you, in you and for you (Emmanuel), now you can see that Jesus Christ is the only friend that can always be there for you. Just like He said in the bible *"And lo I am with you always, even to the end of the world." [Mathew 28:20].* He is the omnipotent (all-ruling) God, the omniscient (all-knowing) God, omnipresent (all present), God.

He has always loved you no matter the height of your sins. He is the ever loving God. He reaches out to the people from every walk of life for the purpose of attaining a personal relationship with them. He did not care if they were rich or poor because his love is equitable. If you can remember from scriptures, He even reached out to a Samaritan woman who others never liked and would ridicule him for having such a relationship, your status in life is not a concern and will never be.

If we can understand that Christ has our love, then we can begin to see that he has our all. It is not until we admit that He has our love, Christ will never have what he deserves from us. True love holds back nothing from Christ when it is sincerely set up on him. If we actually love Christ, He will have our time. He will be at our services, and He will also have the use of all our resources and gifts and grace. He will also indeed have our compassion, freedom and our all, whenever He demands them. In the same way, when God loves any of us, he will never withhold anything good and beautiful from us. Remember God did not even hold back his own only begotten son from dying for our sin. Just like the scripture said, *"He that spared not his own Son, but delivered him up for us all, how shall he not with him also freely gives us all things?" [Romans 8:32].* Christ loves us; that's why he gives us everything we need, his preeminence to justify us in all areas of life, his spirit to consecrate us, his grace to adorn us and his glory, our royal diadem. Therefore, brethren, "when we confess that we love Christ sincerely, it is demanded that we lay the whole thing down at his feet and give up everything at his command and services like it was shown in the book of revelation *"And they loved not their lives unto death" [Revelation 12:11].*

## NEW FRIEND, MEET JESUS CHRIST, THE EVER PERFECT FRIEND

It is quite evident that Christ already knows all about you. When I say all about you I mean your past, present, and your beautiful future, so likewise God in heaven. Remember He is the beginning and the end. He designed and created you. He saw both the fortunate and unfortunate things you have gone through in life. He has been waiting patiently, with all eagerness all, this time, just for you to reach the point where you want a good fellowship restored between you and Him (God the Father, God the Son, God the Holy Spirit) concurring to the original plan. This will only come about when the Holy Spirit of God finds His way into your heart. He intends to make your heart his home since your body is supposed to be a temple of God.

Before I move on, I will like to clarify some few fundamental facts about Jesus Christ. And His place in the Trinity, just so we don't end up bewildering ourselves with the names, titles, and terms used. For the sake of those totally new to this, God, as it was clearly illuminated in the Holy Scriptures, is a spirit. He is the All-Mighty God, creator of the universe, all living and non-living creatures including the stars, planets, human and everything that's not man-made on it. God has always been; he is the beginning and the end, and from the beginning of creation. We have always seen and experienced God in three distinct personalities. He is God the Father who is also the fountainhead of all life. God the Son, Christ who came to reenact our relationship, we lost through Adam in the Garden of Eden, thereby bridging the gap between the father and us. It was His blood that was shed on the cross of Calvary that made us pure, holy and acceptable before Father. That is why we have perfect access to speak directly to the Father. The Holy Spirit, the third person of the Trinity, is the comforter. He comes in after we have determined to accept Christ as our personal Lord and Saviour. His principal duty is to guide, teach and comfort us in everything we do.

It is quite understandable if you are new to this, it has never been an easy endeavor to comprehend the trinity of God. He has and will always make his Son the center of attention. In fact, He wants us to converge all of our interest and activities on his Son. He desires that we elevate him than any person or thin so that all men would venerate him. It is quite fascinating to know that, understanding that aspect of God helps us appreciate the other aspect of God, even though we get our terms mixed up most times while learning about God. He will be glorified and will also glorify himself in us if we can focus our heart and sight on his begotten son, the author and the finisher of our faith, believe and obey all his spoken and written words (Rhema and Logos),

For this reason, even a little child, regardless of age can learn to love Jesus and grow in wisdom, knowledge and clearer understanding of faith.

It's so humanly possible for us to have believed that we have outgrown the need for Jesus when we make friends such as having a life partner, colleagues, friends, associates and so on. It's so imperative to know that God desires and longs to be friends with us far more than we do with him. Just for this reason alone, He sent His only begotten Son to close the gap between the father and us. It is wholly spiritual and therefore invisible, but it vitally affects our lives physically, emotionally and positively. I am a living proof of that.

I will wrap this up with an old song that always ministers to me so dearly. I believe this life touching hymn will bless your soul. It may help affix your mind on Jesus. You may not know the song, but it is very easy to find on youtube.com. It was written by JOSEPH M. SCRIVEN [1857].

## WHAT A FRIEND WE HAVE IN JESUS

1. What a friend we have in Jesus,
All our sins and griefs to bear!
What a privilege to carry
Everything to God in prayer!
O what peace we often forfeit,
O what needless pain we bear,
All because we do not carry
Everything to God in prayer
2. Have we trials and temptations?
Is there trouble anywhere?
We should never be discouraged;
Take it to the Lord in prayer.
Can we find a friend so faithful?
Who will all our sorrows share?
Jesus knows our every weakness;
Take it to the Lord in prayer.

3. Are we weak and heavy laden?
Cumbered with a load of care
Precious Savior, still our refuge;
Take it to the Lord in prayer
Do thy friends despise, forsake thee?
Take it to the Lord in prayer!
In his arms, he'll take and shield thee;
Thou wilt finds a solace there

4. Blessed Savior, Thou hast promised
Thou wilt all our burdens bear
May we ever, Lord, be bringing
all to Thee in earnest prayer.

**Soon in glory bright unclouded
there will be no need for prayer
Rapture, praise and endless worship
will be our sweet portion there.
Words: Joseph Screven (1855)**

## DO YOU WANT TO BECOME FRIEND WITH JESUS TOO?

### HERE IS WHAT MUST HAPPEN

I believe by now you must be entirely confident that you cannot have fellowship with the Holy God, our Creator, the master of the universe by any other way except through his son Jesus Christ. This was clearly stated in the book of John *"Jesus saith unto him, I am the way, the truth, and the life: no man cometh unto the Father, but by me" [John 14:6].* For you to be a friend of Jesus, you must first accept the truth that Jesus died on the cross of Calvary deliberately for our sin's sake. When you feel sure of this, you are instantly redeemed of every erroneous thought about Him. According to the book of Corinthians *"Therefore if any man is in Christ, he is a new creature: old things are passed away; behold, all things are become new" [2 Corinthians 5:17].* God completely washes and cleans every record of sin and guilt connected to your name, don't you think that's breathtaking? It is very understandable that you may or may not have a prodigious sensation of a jam-packed guilt and shame. You may not feel any physical changes right now, since it is a supernatural transaction, that emotions will have to be trained to catch up with the spectral changes. If you find out that your heart still meddles with a tremendous sense of guilt, it may be a great help to let your new friend (Jesus) know how sorry you feel deep inside of you, by confessing any sin you can hark back to. God assured us that If we confess our sins, he is faithful and just to forgive us our sins, and to cleanse us from all unrighteousness" [1 John 1:9]. He also encouraged us to *"Come now, and let us reason together, says the Lord. Though your sins are like scarlet, they shall be as white as snow; though they are red like crimson, they shall be as wool." [Isaiah 1:18AMP]*

To crown this process of redemption, we must also believe that Christ rose from the dead and ascended back to heaven so as to prepare a home for us. For this reason, we can be forgiven, with the empowerment to live holy and acceptable life before God. By the power of His resurrection, Christ helps us to live a righteous life. It will be a great pleasure before God to see you treasure this moment with a helpful prayer of determination, inviting Jesus Christ into your life. You may make your own words as it is from the depth of your heart, but for the sake of those of us that are new to this, you may use this prayer guide, as a model to begin with your own talk with your new friend.

> *Oh Lord Jesus, I duly acknowledge that I've been a sinner against man, myself and God. I clearly understand now that your death on the cross has paid for my sins.*
>
> *I firmly believe that, and so much love and appreciate you for it.*
>
> *I'm extending to you a sincere invitation into my life to be my personal lord and savior,*

*I understand that by receiving you, I also receive eternal life, and I shall live and reign forever in heaven with you.*

*From now henceforth, I want you to be my very best friend!*

*Come dwell inside of me by your Holy Spirit. Kindly allow my body to be the temple of the Holy Spirit.*

*Fill me up with your spirit, Lord Jesus! So I may do great things in your name to glorify you.*

*I want to really know you more and to also find your other friends who can help me with my new friendship with you. "Amen."*

When you are done with your conversation with God, just know that He has seen and heard every word that came out of you. And now you a friend of Jesus! I officially welcome you into this great family.

God has warned us that we should never be ignorant of the devices of the enemy (devil). Satan, of course, is the enemy of God and all believers, he is also the accuser of brethren. He is bent on doing anything in his power to make you doubt your redemption.

All Jesus wants you to do is to constantly tell him what is going on with you. He wants you to depend so much on his name.

Remember *"The name of the LORD is a strong tower: the righteous runneth into it and is safe" [Proverb 18:10].*

I will end this by encouraging you to cheer up. Soon, whether after we have breathed our last breath or if we should live until Jesus comes, he will come and take us home.

For the Lord, himself shall descend from heaven with a shout, with the voice of the unchanged, and with the trump of God, and dead in Christ shall rise first. Then we which are alive and remain shall be caught up together with them in the clouds, to meet the Lord in the air, and so shall we ever be with the Lord [1Thessalonia 4:16-17], we will get to ride on a cloud and with a trumpet blast. We shall get to see him face to face. The joy of the whole matter is that we will have a joyful, trouble-free life and reign in heaven with the King.

**Dear Friend,**

Once again you are now welcome into the big family. It will be a great pleasure to see you write us a letter or send us a mail, sharing with us about yourself and your new friend, Jesus. We will also be glad to hear the testimony of your redemption and what the Lord has been doing in your life. We will love to see you flourish in this new relationship of yours.

> *Beloved, I earnestly pray that it may be well with you in all aspect of life and that you may be in good health, just as just as your soul keeps thriving and prospers.*

Thank you for your time spent on reading this book, am so glad I was able to introduce you to Jesus Christ.

I pray that you will derive much joy and delight in your new relationship with Jesus.

**HAVE A GREAT & BLESSED LIFE!**

# REFERENCES

Crosnoe, R., & Needham, B. (2004). Holism, contextual variability, and the study of friendships in adolescent development. Child development.

"Jonathan and David – A True and Lasting Friendship. The Restored Church of God, Jan. 2013. Web. 03 Oct. 2015.

Scriven, J. M. (n.d.). What a Friend We Have in Jesus. Retrieved September 03, 2015, from http://library.timelesstruths.org/ music/What_a_Friend_We_Have_in_Jesus/.

# NOTES

**Bishop Thomas Dexter Jakes, Jr.**, chief Pastor of "The Potter's House" in Dallas Texas.

**President Barack Hussein Obama II** the 44th and current President of the United States.

**Bishop David O. Oyedepo** is a Nigerian noble author, preacher, the founder and Presiding Bishop of Living Faith Church World Wide.

**William Franklin "Billy" Graham, Jr**. is a well-known American Evangelical Christian evangelist ordained as a Southern Baptist minister.

**William Henry "Bill" Gates III** is a famous American business magnate, philanthropist, investor, computer programmer, and inventor.

Steven **Paul "Steve" Jobs** was a well respected American entrepreneur, marketer, and inventor, who was the co-founder, chairman, and CEO of Apple Inc.

**Warren Edward Buffett** is a distinguished American business magnate, investor, and philanthropist.

**Mark Elliot Zuckerberg** an American computer programmer and Internet entrepreneur. He is the current chairman and C.E.O of Facebook Inc.

For speaking engagements, blogs on current issues, speeches and sermon, articles, inquiry, prayer request, testimony or for more copies, please visit Rev. Ehihi's website @ www.ehihidominion.com.

Also available- information on His True Dominion Inspiration Ministry (HisTDI), write us @ info.@histdi.org or visit www.histdi.org.

## His True Dominion Inspiration Ministry (HisTDI)

### Soaring you to greater heights in life

HisTDI by God's grace is a ministry operating under the leading of God to inspire and transform mankind. Soaring them to greater heights in life with the power and word of God. HisTDI ministry stands by eight core values – Love, Encouragement, Truthful testimonies, Self-motivation, Sacrifice, Obedience, Attitude and Reaching out to others - that help us show how grateful we are to our Lord Jesus for having sacrificed himself for our sins. We strive to create a healthy community that encourages, supports and transforms the lives of everyone. We wish to help you enlighten yourself with His teachings. Keeping in mind the constraints faced by people in this modern age, we have begun a new facility for those who wish to become a part of our family – an e-church. This online service offers Bible study, group Bible study, counseling, prayer, testimony and a live church. Additionally, it also acts as a platform to connect with other members. This e-church was created to enable more people, interested in understanding His teachings with a new perspective, to be able to attend church irrespective of who they are, their location or circumstances. We hope this initiative helps us spread love and power to more people."

HisTDI is poised to be a generational solution to humanity. We hope and believe that since you are here, your life will never remain the same.

Remain Blessed and Inspired.

# ABOUT THE AUTHOR

Rev. Ehihi A. Dominion is the president of His True Dominion Inspiration Ministry. A ministry that is well known to be under God's mandate to soar humanity to greater heights in life with the word and power of God. Aside his degrees in Aviation, he has also earned his B.Sc. in Psychology from Upper Iowa University, and currently undergoing his Masters of Divinity (M.Div.) in Regent University, VA. Recognized as a member of the Honor Society. org. He is the author of so many friends, so little friendship. He has also authored numerous inspirational articles and evangelical pamphlets. Rev. Ehihi's personal experience and current service in the military have led to his enthusiasm and devotion to the continued exploration of the diverse issues of the motivation and inspiration process for a better life.

He is blissfully married to Olubunmi Precious, who currently work together with him in life and ministry.

Printed in the United States
By Bookmasters